CLEVELAND
—— AND THE ——
CIVIL WAR

CLEVELAND
— AND THE —
CIVIL WAR

W. DENNIS KEATING

THE
History
PRESS

Published by The History Press
Charleston, SC
www.historypress.com

Copyright © 2022 by W. Dennis Keating
All rights reserved

First published 2022

Manufactured in the United States

ISBN 9781467147736

Library of Congress Control Number: 2021950604

This history of Cleveland in the Civil War is dedicated to the memory of those Clevelanders and others from Cuyahoga County who served in the Union military forces and who are remembered in the Soldiers' and Sailors' Monument, as well as to the Cleveland Civil War Roundtable (https://www.clevelandcivilwarroundtable.com), which keeps the history of the Civil War alive for interested residents of Northeast Ohio. The Roundtable was founded in 1956. I was honored to be its president in 2009–10.

Contents

Preface   9
Acknowledgements   11
Introduction   13

PRE–CIVIL WAR CLEVELAND
    The 1850s   15
    Cleveland   19
CIVIL WAR
    Politics   31
    Military History   38
    Notable Cleveland Places   108
    The Economy and Population   111
POST–CIVIL WAR CLEVELAND
    The Fenian Invasion of Canada   117
    Reconstruction   118
    Cleveland's Rise as an Industrial City   119
    Mass Immigration   121
    Garfield Memorial   121
    Soldiers' and Sailors' Monument   123
    Grand Army of the Republic   125

Conclusion   127
Bibliography   129
Index   137
About the Author   141

PREFACE

T his book places Cleveland, the surrounding county of Cuyahoga and the nearby town of Oberlin in the Civil War and in The History Press series on the Civil War. Ohio, including these places and their residents—both those in the Union military and civilians—played a very important role in the conflict. Its leaders—including politicians in Columbus and Washington, military officers and leaders of organizations supporting the war effort—played prominent roles in war. There were also many opponents in Ohio who sought the end of the war with the South and slavery intact. With a summary of events leading up to the war and a short history of the postwar period, including Reconstruction, this book captures both major events and the everyday experience of participants.

ACKNOWLEDGEMENTS

This book is the result of a call from John Rodrigue of The History Press asking if I would be interested in doing another book. Finding that its Civil War series did not have a book on Cleveland and as a member and past president of the Cleveland Civil War Roundtable, I suggested that I do that topic. John both agreed and has been an excellent editor during the COVID-19 pandemic, which presented several roadblocks to the completion of this book.

One of the best sources for Civil War manuscripts and photographs is the collection at the Cleveland History Center of the Western Reserve Historical Society. Ann K. Sindelar, its reference supervisor, was instrumental in my gaining access when it was limited by the pandemic and in helping me find documents and photographs that I wanted to review.

Another excellent local resource for information related to Cleveland's history is the Cleveland Memory Project at the Cleveland State University Library. I was assisted in using this resource by William C. Barrow, director of its special collections, and Elizabeth Piwkowski.

Two other Ohio institutions were also important in my research. The Oberlin College Library's Civil War Archives had valuable information and photos about Oberlin College students who served in Cleveland-based regiments. Archivist Ken M. Grossi was most helpful in my using this data. The Columbus-based Ohio History Connection has a vast collection of Civil War photos, including many related to Cleveland and Northern Ohio. Jen Cabiya, its digital projects coordinator, helped in my accessing some of those photos.

Beyond these Ohio institutions, I also was able to use photos from the Civil War Collection of the Prints & Photographic Division of the Library of Congress.

Several individuals also helped me with photographic information. Cleveland historian Chris Roy shared his photos of Camp Cleveland and other local scenes. Michelle Day, head of the Woodland Cemetery Foundation, helped me in learning about that important part of Cleveland's Civil War history. And fellow Civil War buff and History Press author Jim Madden provided me with a photo of Thomas Francis Galwey of Cleveland's Hibernian Guards and the 8th Ohio Volunteer Infantry, who is featured in the book.

I asked several knowledgeable individuals to review my draft manuscripts and received their very helpful feedback. They were John J. Grabowski of the Western Reserve Historical Society and Case Western Reserve University and some fellow members of the Cleveland Civil War Roundtable: Ellen C. Connally, Dave Carrino, Paul Siedel and William F.B. Vodrey.

Finally, my wife, Kay Martin, was both an invaluable reviewer and copy editor of my work as it evolved and also a photographer who shot photos of several key Cleveland and Oberlin Civil War sites.

INTRODUCTION

Cleveland, Ohio, was a city transformed by the American Civil War. From its growth before the war with the opening of a canal and then the arrival of railroads, it boomed during the bloody conflict. Before the war, Cleveland politically had become a stronghold of Republicans, including abolitionists. It was a station on the Underground Railroad for escaped slaves. It voted to elect (and reelect) Abraham Lincoln as president of the United States. With the outbreak of the war, its residents largely supported Lincoln's resolve to save the Union and end the rebellion of the states of the Confederacy.

Thousands of Clevelanders enlisted in the Union's army and navy and served in Ohio's many infantry and cavalry regiments and artillery batteries. This book recounts the history of the battles and campaigns in which a select number of these units fought. It highlights the experiences of select volunteer officers and enlisted soldiers, especially those from Cleveland. The views of citizen soldiers are captured in their wartime letters and diaries. This history also illustrates the efforts of Cleveland's citizens and civic organizations to support the troops from the homefront.

Major events before, during and after the war are described. Many notable Clevelanders are profiled. These include John D. Rockefeller, who rose to become a prosperous businessman on the path to wealth, fame and controversy as the creator of Standard Oil, and James Garfield, who rose from poverty to political prominence, becoming the twentieth president of the United States, only to be assassinated shortly after taking office.

Places such as Public Square, two important cemeteries and the wartime Camp Cleveland, all of which played important roles, are also profiled. Civil War monuments such as the Soldiers' and Sailors' Monument, which commemorates Civil War veterans from Cuyahoga County, including Cleveland, and other important wartime figures are also identified. Levi Schofield, the designer of the Soldiers' and Sailors' Monument, was a Civil War veteran. Another major monument is the James Garfield Memorial.

Ohio's wartime governors and Cleveland's wartime mayors are profiled. Local Cleveland history often intertwines with national events, such as the 1864 presidential election and the April 1865 assassination of Abraham Lincoln by John Wilkes Booth. As Lincoln's body was returned home, his funeral train stopped in Cleveland. Cleveland's postwar rise as an industrial city and the arrival of European immigrants to work in its factories is explained. Finally, Union veterans of the Grand Army of the Republic met three times in Cleveland during the national organization's history.

Pre–Civil War Cleveland

The 1850s

In order to understand Cleveland's history as an antislavery center and a Republican-voting city entering the Civil War, it is necessary to know about the many major events, some violent, that led up to the election of Republican Abraham Lincoln as president in 1860 and the subsequent secession of the southern states that formed the Confederacy, resulting in the Civil War. While this is a very complicated decade of both conflict and compromise, the following is a concise review of these major events—many of which occurred far from the city of Cleveland but nevertheless impacted its citizens (and the rest of the nation).

The Compromise of 1850/Fugitive Slave Act

In 1820, a compromise was reached by Congress in an attempt to limit the extension of slavery, protected by the Constitution, beyond a stated northern boundary. However, with the vast territories ceded by Mexico to the United States in the treaty that ended the Mexican-American War, the issue arose again. President Polk had initiated this war with the aim of expanding proslavery territory. There was opposition to this war, including by Abraham Lincoln, an obscure new Whig congressman from Illinois.

In 1850, Congress reached another compromise, championed by Senator Henry Clay of Kentucky. It admitted California, which banned slavery, as a free state. However, it opened the possibility of slavery being allowed in the New Mexico and Utah territories. It also included the Fugitive Slave Act, mandating citizen cooperation in returning escaped slaves to their owners. It became known as the "Bloodhound Act" and met with considerable northern opposition. While the slave trade was banned in Washington City, slavery was still allowed in the nation's capital.

Harriet Beecher Stowe's Uncle Tom's Cabin (1852)

Shortly after passage of this legislation, Harriet Beecher Stowe published the antislavery novel *Uncle Tom's Cabin*. She was the daughter of Henry Beecher, a nationally known abolitionist. Stowe said that her best-selling novel was based on her experience while living in Cincinnati, Ohio, as James Bissland noted:

> *There was what Southerners referred to as "that book." From what Harriet Beecher Stowe saw of slavery's fleeing victims while she was living in Ohio came her powerful novel* Uncle Tom's Cabin, *in 1852. With its iconic image of Eliza fleeing over the ice floes—Ohio River ice floes, in fact—the book aroused Northern sympathy for the slaves like nothing before—a turning point. Southerners resented the book. Also angering them and increasingly energizing the North were those who were conducting the Underground Railroad. Ohio's "system" for helping escaped slaves escape was the largest west of the Appalachians.*

Kansas-Nebraska Act (Bleeding Kansas)/Republican Party (1854)

In 1854, Illinois Democratic senator Stephen Douglas, seeking to win support for a presidential nomination in 1856, reopened the slavery issue. He proposed to create territorial governments for Kansas and Nebraska with the provision that their settlers themselves could vote to decide whether to allow slavery. This "Popular Sovereignty" policy overruled the Missouri Compromise. It sparked what became known as "Bleeding Kansas" as proslavery and antislavery settlers fought over the status of slavery in that territory. It led to the creation of competing governments and violence (including by that led by abolitionist John Brown).

That same year, a new political party emerged with the demise of the Whig Party. It was composed of antislavery "Free Soilers," former members of the anti-Catholic "Know Nothing" American party and former Whigs (including Abraham Lincoln). The Republican Party opposed the extension of slavery into the new territories but was not in favor of the abolition of slavery.

U.S. Senate: Brooks's Attack on Sumner, John Brown's Pottawatomie Massacre and the Presidential Election (1856)

Charles Sumner from Massachusetts was a leading abolitionist in the U.S. Senate. He was a strong opponent of the Kansas-Nebraska Act and its sponsor, Stephen Douglas. In a two-day speech in May 1856, Sumner attacked not only Douglas but also Democratic senator Andrew Butler of South Carolina. In response, Preston Brooks, a South Carolina congressman and cousin of Butler, entered the Senate chamber and viciously attacked Sumner, who never fully recovered, with his cane. While the North was appalled, the South applauded Brooks's act.

In November 1837, abolitionist journalist Elijah Lovejoy was murdered by a mob of his proslavery enemies in Alton, Illinois. When news of his murder reached the village of Hudson in Northern Ohio, John Brown took a fateful oath. Brown and his growing family had been forced by his bankruptcy in the financial crisis that year to move back there, where his father lived. Brown rose up in a Congregational church and declared, "Here, before God, in the presence of these witnesses, from this time I consecrate my life to the destruction of slavery."

In 1856, John Brown went to Kansas to join the Free Staters. On May 24, together with four of his sons and two others, they went to the Pottawatomie Creek settlement and killed five proslavery settlers. This massacre gained Brown national notoriety among proponents of both sides.

That fall, the new Republican Party nominated its first presidential candidate: John C. Frémont, a western explorer known as the "Pathfinder." An antislavery candidate, Frémont lost to Democrat James Buchanan. Frémont would go on to play controversial roles in the Civil War.

U.S. Supreme Court's Dred Scott Decision (1857)

Dred Scott, a slave, claimed that by his owner taking him into "free" U.S. states, he could not be reenslaved. In a complicated case, Scott lost his appeal to the Missouri Supreme Court. When Scott appealed to the federal courts, it was heard by the U.S. Supreme Court, led by Marylander and former slave owner Roger Taney. In a 7-2 decision, Taney wrote the opinion of the majority. Instead of simply deciding that Scott was not a citizen and had no standing to bring his lawsuit, Taney went beyond this narrow legal point. He ruled that since slaves were property, their owners could not be stopped from holding and owning them anywhere in the United States. Taney's opinion repealed the previous Congressional attempts at compromise on the extension of slavery and arguably was a major cause of the Civil War.

Lincoln-Douglas Illinois Senatorial Debates (1858)

In 1858, Illinois senator Stephen Douglas was challenged for reelection by Springfield Republican lawyer and state representative Abraham Lincoln. The campaign's highlight was a series of debates around the state over the slavery issue. Douglas tried to paint Lincoln as an abolitionist. While Lincoln forcefully stated his opposition to slavery and its extension, he also respected the Constitution's protection of slavery where it then existed. While Lincoln lost this election, it established him as a national political figure.

John Brown's Harper's Ferry Raid (1859)

In 1859, John Brown activated his audacious plan to provoke a slave uprising that he hoped would lead to the end of slavery in the United States. In October, he led a small armed band across the Potomac River to seize the federal arsenal in Harper's Ferry, Virginia, and arm slaves. His attack was quickly defeated, and he was executed. The raid enraged the South. Following Brown's death, he was praised as a martyr by many in the North. Northern troops in the Civil War would sing the song "John Brown's Body," converted by poet Julia Ward Howe into "Battle Hymn of the Republic," in his memory.

CLEVELAND

Settlement, Canals and Railroads

Cleveland is located in the region once governed by the Northwest Ordinance of 1787, which banned slavery. Its location bordering the southern states of Virginia and Kentucky would be important to the outcome of the Civil War. In 1796, Moses Cleaveland of Connecticut led a party to survey its Western Reserve lands in what was then largely a wilderness. The surveying party chose the confluence of the Cuyahoga River with Lake Erie to establish a settlement. Cleaveland laid out the site for this settlement and never returned to the town that was named for him. This settlement grew very slowly until its future as a commercial center was influenced by the opening of the Erie Canal in 1825. That enabled producers of goods bound for eastern markets to ship freight from Cleveland by the lake to Buffalo and then by the canal to New York City and other destinations.

With the success of the Erie Canal, the small city of Cleveland grew, and like its counterparts, it also wanted a canal to connect to the hinterland for the easier shipment of goods. In 1827, the Ohio & Erie Canal opened, with its northern terminus in Cleveland, thanks to the efforts of Alfred Kelley, the first mayor of Cleveland village, and with its southern landing located on the Ohio River. The canal gave impetus to Cleveland's commercial growth as well as population growth from the canal builders, many of them immigrants. One of the canal's barge drivers was a young James Garfield, future president of the United States, who survived malaria from falling into the canal. In 1851, railroads arrived in Cleveland, connecting it first to Columbus and Cincinnati and then to Pittsburgh. When, in 1853, Cleveland became a hub for trains connecting New York City with Chicago, its commerce grew more through the railroads, which eventually doomed the Ohio & Erie Canal as a major factor in trade through Cleveland.

The year 1859 saw several significant economic events take place. The Lake Erie Iron Ore Company added a rolling mill to make bar iron. Under the new name of Otis & Company, it became a major supplier of railroad iron and gun carriage axles to the Union during the Civil War. On August 27, E.L. Drake struck oil near Titusville, Pennsylvania. Oil and oil refining would play a major role in Cleveland's rise as an industrial city in the coming years. Earlier that year, an ambitious clerk named John D. Rockefeller formed a partnership with Maurice B. Clark to start a produce commission business. This began his rise to commercial success during the Civil War.

During the 1850s, the population of Cleveland increased by more than two and a half times to 43,417 in 1860. On the eve of the Civil War, Cleveland was a bustling commercial city, as described by Van Tassel and Vacha:

In 1860 the Port of Cleveland at the mouth of the Cuyahoga River was a forest of masts and twisted ropes, with the lake schooners, steamboats, scows, and canal barges crowding the river beyond the terminus of the Ohio Canal at the end of Superior Street and around the sharp horseshoe bend in the river. The noise of the busy shipping area was loud, a combination of clanking steam engines, the hiss of escaping steam, the shouts of stevedores and sailors, as docking, unloading, and onloading went on ceaselessly throughout the day. The wail of train whistles and the clanging of bells added to the din with their announcement of the arrival and departure of passenger and freight trains to or from the wooden depots of six railroad lines concentrated in the port area.

The Oberlin-Wellington Rescue

Under the terms of the Northwest Ordinance of 1787 governing the Western Reserve and then the new state of Ohio, slavery was prohibited. With increasing conflict in the country during the Mexican-American War and following the Compromise of 1850, which included the revised and more draconian Fugitive Slave Act, Ohio became a major player in national events. Sympathetic Ohioans aided escaped slaves to reach Canada by what became known as the Underground Railroad. With the publication in 1852 of the novel *Uncle Tom's Cabin* by Harriet Beecher Stowe based on her experiences while living in Cincinnati, the antislavery movement grew both in numbers and passion in the North.

Under the law, however, the federal government as well as northern states were bound to allow slavecatchers to operate within their territory. Escaped slaves crossed the Ohio River and then made their way north, usually aiming to cross the U.S. border into Canada. As a gateway to Canada across Lake Erie, Cleveland was an antislavery stronghold. In Cleveland, St. John's Episcopal Church in Ohio City was reputedly a station on the Underground Railroad. Its code name was "Station Hope." In January 1854, abolitionist members of the Disciples of Christ held an antislavery convention in Cleveland.

The year 1854 saw the birth of the new Republican Party opposed to the extension of slavery. The year 1855 saw the victory of Cincinnati lawyer

Salmon P. Chase as its candidate for governor of Ohio. His election was celebrated on Cleveland's Public Square on October 13 with a 101-gun salute, fireworks, a parade and a giant bonfire.

Antislavery speakers like Reverend Henry Ward Beecher and Frederick Douglass lectured in Cleveland. Douglass spoke in Cleveland on January 15–16, 1863, shortly after President Lincoln issued the Emancipation Proclamation, according to Van Tassel and Vacha:

> *The Emancipation Proclamation, published in the local newspapers on Saturday, January 3, 1863, galvanized the local black community into joyful action and rekindled the debate between the Republican newspapers, the* Herald *and the* Leader *and the Democratic* Plain Dealer, *which would continue into the fall through the bitter and acrimonious gubernatorial election….A capacity crowd paid twenty-five cents admission to hear America's most renowned former slave* [on January 15].…*He repeated his remarks the following night at a jubilee organized by Cleveland's "colored citizens" in National Hall. "The night was stormy, and pedestrianism difficult on account of the deep snow, yet the hall was packed," noted the* Leader. *Behind the speakers were "two full length portraits of an African," one depicting him in chains and the other with broken shackles at his side and hands uplifted in thanks toward heaven. Looming above the stage was a portrait of John Brown. Before speaking, Douglass asked the assembly to arise in singing "The Year of Jubilee Has Come." Among the other speakers were two black men from Oberlin. Former rescuer John Watson recited a firsthand account of the Oberlin-Wellington Rescue that had so stirred northern Ohio four years earlier. He was followed by J.M. Langston "who consumed much of his time advocating the right and duty of colored men to stand on the battlefield alongside of their pale-faced brethren, and fight against the enemies of their country, for it is their country now."*

Oberlin was a hotbed of abolitionism. It was a small town west of Cleveland. Oberlin College (originally named the Oberlin Collegiate Institute) was founded there in 1833. After heated debates among its students and trustees, the trustees agreed by a 5-4 vote in the following year to admit students "irrespective of color." By the spring of 1859, there were 32 Black students among a total of about 1,200 students. Among Oberlin's Black students was Rosetta Douglass, the daughter of Frederick Douglass. Oberlin College's unusual position in admitting Black students brought criticism and four attempts by Democrat-controlled state legislatures to repeal its charter.

Left: Frederick Douglass. *Courtesy of Library of Congress.*

Below: Oberlin-Wellington Rescuers. *Courtesy of Oberlin College Civil War Archives.*

Several Underground Railroad routes ran through Oberlin, and some of the Oberlin College students and townspeople aided Black men and women to escape from slavecatchers. In the 1860 federal census, the town of Oberlin recorded 2,114 "free inhabitants," of whom 416 were Black.

In 1858, Oberlin's antislavery reputation on the issue of slavery soared in Ohio and nationally. By late summer, three attempts by slave hunters had been foiled. Then three slavecatchers from Kentucky arrived in Oberlin to capture a man named John Price, who had escaped from a farm there four years earlier. After capturing Price on September 13, they turned him over to the U.S. marshal for Northern Ohio, who then took Price to the nearby town of Wellington to catch a train to Columbus. When this news was heard, many residents of Oberlin rushed to Wellington, where they were joined by others from nearby communities. Eventually, hundreds surrounded the hotel where Price was being held. After failed negotiations, members of the crowd stormed the building and freed Price, returning him to Oberlin and a celebration of his freedom. He was then hidden in the home of James H. Fairchild, an Oberlin College professor and a future president of the college. Later, Price was led to refuge in Canada.

On December 6, a federal grand jury indicted thirty-seven rescuers, including twelve free Blacks, for violating the Fugitive Slave Act—twenty-five from Oberlin and twelve from Wellington.

Their trials were held in the new Cuyahoga County Courthouse in downtown Cleveland. Representing the rescuers were Rufus Spalding and Albert Riddle, both friends of Ohio Republican governor Salmon Chase and both antislavery. The trial of the first rescuer, printer Simeon Bushnell, began on April 5, 1859. Bushnell had previously been represented by Rufus Spalding in 1859 for violating the Fugitive Slave Act. Spalding argued that the act was unconstitutional. Before a jury packed with Democrats and a federal judge known to be anti-abolitionist, the verdict was not in doubt, and the jury convicted Bushnell on April 15. One of the visitors who attended Bushnell's trial was John Brown, the notorious antislavery firebrand. The rest of the jailed rescuers were to be freed on bail awaiting their trial, but twenty protesting Oberlin rescuers refused to be released. Their confinement was friendly due to a sympathetic sheriff and jailer, and they were allowed to receive visitors. Their cause not only was supported by numerous local citizens but also now received national attention.

At the beginning of the trial of a second rescuer, Charles Langston, a mixed-race schoolteacher and officer of the Ohio State Anti-Slavery Society, the next dramatic event occurred. After testifying against Langston, two

Oberlin-Wellington Rescue Monument. *Photo by Kay L. Martin.*

of the Kentucky slavecatchers were arrested in the courtroom by a local sheriff and charged under Ohio law with kidnapping Price. After the trial proceeded, Langston, too, was convicted.

On May 24, 1858, a huge crowd of supporters of the jailed rescuers arrived in Cleveland to surround the jail and protest the prosecutions. The Oberlin delegation was led by the Oberlin Brass Band. The crowd was addressed by Langston and other rescuers and also by other speakers, including Ohio governor Chase. Led by Ohio's attorney general, the next step was an attempt to have the Ohio Supreme Court release the jailed rescuers under the Ohio Constitution. However, by a vote of 3-2, the court rejected this attempt on May 30.

While the slavecatchers posted bail, Langston completed his sentence, leaving thirteen Oberlin rescuers still jailed. Unknown to them, a deal was reached to drop the charges against them in return for the kidnappers escaping the charges against them. On July 6, the last of the rescuers finally left the jail to a celebration, including cannon fire and bands playing as they caught the train back to Oberlin. Bushnell was later released on July 11.

John Brown's Harper's Ferry Raid

In 1858, John Brown was planning a momentous event: a slave uprising in Virginia to begin the death of slavery in the United States. His target was the capture of the federal arsenal at Harper's Ferry, Virginia, to arm a slave army. In March 1858, a group of supporters (the "Secret Six") formed to raise funding for Brown's plan. In August 1859, Frederick Douglass was summoned to meet with John Brown in Chambersburg, Pennsylvania. Accompanied by runaway slave Shields Green from South Carolina, whom Douglass had befriended, they listened as Brown tried to persuade them to join him. Brown had first explained his plan to Douglass in an 1847 meeting. While Douglass tried to talk Brown out of proceeding with his attack, Green agreed to join him. Brown attracted twenty others to join him at a farmhouse across the Potomac from Harper's Ferry.

John Brown Jr. recruited two of the Oberlin rescuers (harness maker Lewis Leary and former Oberlin student John Copeland) to join in his father's raid on Harper's Ferry. It began on October 16, 1859, and quickly ended with most of the raiders killed (including two of John Brown's sons) or captured by U.S. marines led by future Confederate Civil War generals Robert E. Lee and J.E.B. Stuart. Three others who appeared in the aftermath of Brown's

Harper's Ferry Memorial, Oberlin, Ohio. *Photo by Kay L. Martin.*

failed raid would later also play prominent roles in the Civil War. One of three congressmen who interrogated the captured John Brown was Clement Vallandigham of Dayton, Ohio. Present at Brown's execution by hanging on December 2, 1859, were Thomas Jackson, an instructor at the Virginia Military Institute, and actor John Wilkes Booth.

Of the two Oberlin-related Black members of Brown's party, Leary was mortally wounded, and Copeland was captured and executed following John Brown's hanging. There is a monument to them in a park in Oberlin.

Leary's widow, Mary, married Charles Langston (another Oberlin rescuer). Her grandson was poet Langston Hughes, who spent part of his early years in Cleveland, attending Central High School (also attended by John D. Rockefeller and Mark Hanna). In 1931, he wrote a poem titled "October the Sixteenth," ending, "You will recall John Brown."

The Capture of Sara Lucy Bagby

On January 1861, a fugitive slave named Sara Lucy Bagby was captured in Cleveland by a slavecatcher. She had worked as a domestic servant in the home of Republican congressman Albert G. Riddle. Clevelanders again protested against enforcement of the Fugitive Slave Act. William E. Ambush, the chairman of the Fugitive Aid Society, attempted to buy her freedom from her owner, but his offer was refused. This time, despite a sympathetic judge, she was returned to her owner in (West) Virginia after an attempted rescue failed. Bagby was the last escaped slave from Ohio to be returned under the Fugitive Slave Act. When Union forces captured Wheeling, Bagby was freed. In October 1863, Bagby returned to Cleveland and was welcomed by abolitionists, who held a grand jubilee. She died in 1906 and is buried at Woodland Cemetery. Until 2010, her grave was unmarked. Her headstone, installed that year by the cemetery's foundation, reads, "Unfettered and Free."

Sara Lucy Bagby gravestone, Woodland Cemetery, Cleveland, Ohio. *Photo by Kay L. Martin.*

Rufus Spalding, who helped found the Republican Party of Cuyahoga County and defended the Oberlin-Wellington Rescuers and Sara Lucy Bagby, was elected to Congress in 1862. Spalding came to Cleveland in 1852. He previously served as Speaker of the Ohio House of Representatives and as an associate justice of the Ohio Supreme Court. He served throughout the rest of the Civil War. Spalding was one of the congressmen chosen to meet the Lincoln funeral train in Springfield, Illinois, in May 1865.

Dedication of the Perry Monument

Another major event occurred on September 10, 1860, when a monument on Cleveland's Public Square was dedicated to the memory of Oliver Hazard Perry, the victor of the Battle of Lake Erie in the War of 1812. A large crowd was joined by bands and military units from all over Ohio. Later, after a conflict reaching the Ohio Supreme Court over ownership of Public Square, the Perry Monument was relocated elsewhere in downtown Cleveland to make way for the construction of the Soldiers' and Sailors' Monument long after the Civil War.

President-Elect Lincoln's Visit

The year 1860 saw one of the most contentious presidential elections in U.S. history. Four candidates sought the presidency, with Illinois lawyer Abraham Lincoln representing the Republican Party and Illinois senator Stephen Douglas the Democratic Party. The Democratic Party split in two, first over the slavery issue and then over Lincoln's election and his war policy. Two years earlier, Douglas and Lincoln had held a series of debates that included the question of slavery and its future while competing for the Senate seat that Douglas won. But they made Lincoln a national political figure. Most southerners viewed Lincoln as a threat to their economic and social structure based on slavery, but even in the North Lincoln had detractors, including Democrats in Cleveland, as Van Tassel and Vacha noted:

> *Cleveland, long dominated by the Democrats, was now overwhelmingly Republican as Whigs, Free Soilers, and Know-Nothings moved into the city and joined forces in the mid-1850s. Edwin Cowles, bellicose editor of the* Leader, *was one of the founders of the Republican Party in Cuyahoga County and an early supporter of Abraham Lincoln for President....Joseph*

Gray, Democratic editor of the Plain Dealer *and supporter of Senator Stephen A. Douglas, Lincoln's old Illinois rival, reported the split of the Democratic Party as a delegate to the failed Charleston, South Carolina convention and the reconstituted northern Democratic Convention meeting in Baltimore, where Gray finally saw his candidate nominated. The ensuing campaign was bitter, nasty, and blatantly racist.*

Edwin Cowles arrived in Cleveland in 1839 as a printing apprentice, later forming a printing firm. He became the owner of the *Cleveland Leader* newspaper. It printed its first edition on March 16, 1854. Cowles was a leader of the Republican Party in Cleveland and at a meeting in Cleveland helped organize its first national convention. Cowles was antislavery and a strong supporter of President Abraham Lincoln. He was rewarded with the position of Cleveland's postmastership, which he held throughout the Civil War.

Lincoln won the four-way presidential race of 1860 but only with northern votes and a plurality of the votes cast. Lincoln won Ohio with 51.24 percent of the popular vote versus 43.30 percent for Democrat Stephen A. Douglas. In Cuyahoga County, his margin of victory was greater: 62.45 percent versus 34.61 percent for Douglas. Lincoln carried nine of Cleveland's eleven wards with 58 percent of the total vote. Gray would continue to be an ardent opponent of Lincoln while he was the editor of the *Plain Dealer* during the war.

As Van Tassel and Vacha described, Republicans and pro-war Democrats in Cleveland had formed a Union Party to support Lincoln and his wartime policies, which included the Union army's recruitment of Black soldiers beginning in 1863 despite

[the] *charges and fears inflamed by the Democratic press and the Copperhead gubernatorial campaign of Clement L. Vallandigham, which charged that Negroes were inherently undisciplined and would make terrible soldiers and disgrace the flag. Once armed, it was further alleged, they would become predatory marauders against white communities. The race card was blatantly played in the mid-nineteenth century. There could be few worse offenders than the* Cleveland Plain Dealer *in whipping up racial hatred and fear. During the election of 1860, editor Joseph Gray had never missed a chance to portray the Republicans as the party whose victory would lead to the end of slavery and the beginning of racial equality.…Yet Gray, unlike his successor John S. Stephenson, was a shrewd newspaper*

man who had kept the Plain Dealer *solvent as a Democratic organ in a Whig, and then Republican-dominated region. Even after the death of his political icon Stephen A. Douglas in 1861, Gray continued to uphold Douglas' policy in the* Plain Dealer *of supporting the Union while opposing the Republicans.*

Following Lincoln's election, South Carolina voted to secede and left the Union on December 24, 1860. Before Lincoln headed for Washington City to assume office, six more Southern states also voted to secede. Lincoln then faced the greatest political crisis in the history of the young republic.

On February 11, 1861, president-elect Abraham Lincoln left Springfield, Illinois, on a train that would take him to Washington City for his inauguration. His trip was taken against the background of the formation of a Confederacy of seceded Southern states. Lincoln planned many stops in cities along the way in order to present himself to much of the American population. His fifth stop was in Cleveland on February 15, arriving from Pittsburgh. Two miles from Cleveland, Lincoln switched to a carriage that took him to the city, where he was first greeted in falling snow by a crowd of thirty thousand. Lincoln was then escorted to the Weddell House hotel (later replaced in part by John D. Rockefeller as his office building) by the Cleveland Grays, the local militia, amid fire companies and marching bands, to be greeted by thousands more Clevelanders. Lincoln spoke briefly to the crowd from the hotel balcony. To the strains of "Hail Columbia," Lincoln's train departed the next morning headed for Buffalo. Lincoln wouldn't return to Cleveland until April 28, 1865, when his body was carried by his funeral train returning to Springfield for burial.

CIVIL WAR

POLITICS

During the Civil War, Ohio's politics were very divisive. With the birth of the Republican Party and Lincoln's election in 1860, the Democratic Party split into two factions. The War Democrats supported Lincoln. Many, including some of the state's wartime antislavery and formerly Democratic governors and Cleveland mayors, switched to the Republican Party and supported Lincoln's war policies. Democrats opposed to Lincoln were generally known as Peace Democrats or "Copperheads."

Cleveland Mayors during the Civil War

During the Civil War, Cleveland had four mayors, all businessmen. Edward Sherrill was the city's mayor in 1861. Born in Warren, Ohio, he came to Cleveland in 1851 from Vermont, and beginning in 1859, he was superintendent of the Columbus, Cincinnati & Indianapolis Railroad until 1878. Elected to the Cleveland School Board in 1860, he was elected mayor the following year as a Republican who later became a War Democrat. He was defeated for a second term by Irvine Masters. Masters also arrived in Cleveland in 1851, from New York. He was elected to the Cleveland City Council and was its president three times, and when Lincoln visited Cleveland in 1861, Masters officially greeted him. Due to poor health,

Masters resigned in May 1864. George B. Senter was elected by the Cleveland City Council to serve out the rest of Masters's term. Senter, too, came to Cleveland from New York and had previously been mayor, elected in 1859. From 1862 to 1864, Senter was commandant of Camp Taylor in Cleveland. It was Cleveland's first Civil War military camp and was located on the fairgrounds of the Cuyahoga County Agricultural Society. In 1861, the 7th and 8th Ohio Volunteer Infantry and 2nd Ohio Cavalry regiments used it for training. After serving out the rest of Masters's term as mayor, Senter practiced law and had a wine and liquor business. The fourth Cleveland Civil War mayor was Herman M. Chapin. Born in New Hampshire, Chapin arrived in Cleveland in 1848 as a partner in a wholesale grocery warehouse. In 1852, he began his own business as a beef and pork packer. In 1862, he moved to Chicago but later returned to Cleveland. In 1854, Chapin built the Chapin Block at Public Square. He was also president of the Cleveland Library Association.

Ohio's Civil War Governors

In 1859, Salmon Chase went from being the Republican governor of Ohio to the U.S. Senate. When Abraham Lincoln chose his cabinet in March 1861, he chose Chase to be his treasury secretary, a member of his team of rivals. His successor as Ohio's governor was William Dennison, a Cincinnati lawyer, banker, president of a railroad and a founder of the Republican Party. When Chase left the Senate, Dennison sought his seat, but instead the legislature chose John Sherman (brother of General William Tecumseh Sherman). This left Dennison to govern Ohio at the beginning of the Civil War. In May 1861, Dennison went to Cleveland and met with the governors of Indiana, Michigan, Pennsylvania and Wisconsin, as well as representatives from Illinois and New York. They agreed to support whatever measures President Lincoln undertook to suppress the rebellion of the Southern Confederacy. One day after this Cleveland conference, President Lincoln issued a call for forty regiments of three-year volunteers, to be provided by the states. To organize Ohio's militia, Dennison appointed George B. McClellan. During his term (1860–62), Dennison raised more than 100,000 troops for the Union.

Dennison worried about the possibility of the border state of Kentucky also seceding, and he met with the governors of Indiana and Illinois to discuss policies to keep Kentucky at least neutral. Lincoln would later declare that to win the war, he must have Kentucky remain in the Union. Dennison also wanted to support the Unionists in western Virginia (who would lead the secession of that area to create the state of West Virginia, which would be liberated militarily by troops, including those from Ohio led by McClellan). In September 1861, Ohio Republicans formed a "Union" political coalition with pro-war Democrats. Instead of re-nominating Dennison, this Union coalition chose as its gubernatorial candidate David Tod in 1862. This would not be the end of Dennison's political career, however. President Lincoln made Dennison postmaster general.

David Tod was from Youngstown. He was a lawyer, a founder of the iron industry in Youngstown, a president of the Cleveland and Mahoning Railroad and a member of the state senate. He was originally a supporter of Illinois senator Stephen A. Douglas and chaired the Baltimore convention of Democrats that nominated Douglas for president in 1860. He then became a pro-war Democrat after Lincoln's election and the secession of the Southern states. In reaction to Lincoln's Emancipation Proclamation, the Democrats swept the midterm elections in the fall of 1862.

In the late summer of 1862, Confederates invaded Kentucky. Fearing an attack on Cincinnati, General Lew Wallace was sent to organize a defense of the "Queen City." Governor Tod welcomed Ohioans to join in its defense. Thousands (called the "Squirrel Hunters") arrived in the city under martial law, declared by Wallace. However, the Confederate threat to Cincinnati vanished after its invasion of Kentucky ended when the forces under Generals Braxton Bragg and Kirby Smith withdrew after the Battle of Perryville in October. In July 1863, Tod had to mobilize troops to defeat the Southern Ohio Confederate raid led by General John Hunt Morgan.

Tod also had to deal with the criticism of the Peace Democrats and some resistance to the federal draft. In a close vote, the Union Republicans rejected Tod for re-nomination as their gubernatorial candidate in favor of pro-war Democrat John Brough, according to Richard Abbott:

> *Tod was in ill health as he closed out his administration. Governing the state of Ohio through two years of war had worn him out; he had worked hard to fulfill the obligations of his office. Although he, as Brough, had been elected more for his political qualifications than for his executive ability, Tod had demonstrated considerable capability in meeting the problems of raising and providing for state troops. He had dutifully served the cause of the Lincoln administration, a fact that the President recognized.*

Despite Tod's health concerns, Lincoln nominated him in 1864 to succeed Salmon Chase as his treasury secretary, but Radical Republicans in the Senate opposed Tod's nomination. He then withdrew, citing his poor health.

John Brough was involved in running railroads, becoming president of the Indianapolis, Pittsburgh & Cleveland Railroad. He was a Democrat who opposed Lincoln's candidacy in the 1860 election. But he became a pro-war Republican. In the fall 1863 election, he was opposed by Peace Democrat and former congressman Clement Vallandigham. In a June 8, 1863 speech in Cleveland, Brough denounced slavery, while also warning that Ohioans would never accept Vallandigham. When he learned that Brough was elected, President Lincoln exulted, "Glory to God in the Highest, Ohio has saved the nation." In the 1864 presidential election, Brough supported Lincoln, opposing the effort of Salmon Chase to replace Lincoln. In November 1864, Lincoln won Ohio, and the Republicans swept the Congressional election. In the spring of 1865, Brough declined re-nomination, and on August 29, 1865, Ohio's third and last Civil War governor died. These three wartime governors are commemorated in Cleveland's Soldiers' and Sailors' Monument.

The 1864 Election

In the midst of the Civil War, President Abraham Lincoln faced reelection in November 1864. Lincoln feared that he would be defeated in the war-weary Union part of the divided nation. In the face of U.S. Grant's attempted coordinated federal military strategy aimed primarily at the destruction of Robert E. Lee's army of Northern Virginia and the capture of Atlanta, Georgia, by William Tecumseh Sherman's armies, the Confederate strategy was to hold out until Lincoln lost the election. Ohio would play an important role in the election campaign and Cleveland a minor role.

The Peace Democrats favored a negotiated end to the war without emancipation. Their most renowned advocate was the lawyer and former Ohio congressman Clement Vallandigham from Dayton, who was an adamant White supremacist and opponent of the abolitionists. After a speech denouncing Lincoln as a tyrant, he was arrested on May 5, 1863, tried and convicted by a military commission for treason and sentenced to imprisonment for the duration of the war. However, Lincoln did not want Vallandigham seen as a political martyr by the Peace Democrats. He exiled him to the South. This was short-lived because Vallandigham was not welcome there, and he eventually landed in Canada.

From there, he ran for governor of Ohio in October 1863 but was soundly defeated by Republican John Brough in a landslide. The Union soldier vote was a significant factor. In Cuyahoga County, only 8 of 1,141 Union soldiers voted for Vallandigham. Of the 191 members of the 8th Ohio Volunteer Infantry who voted, there was only a single vote for Vallandigham. Dale Thomas noted that Nathan Hawkins of the 103rd OVI was angered by the Ohio Copperheads (a derisive name given to Peace Democrats like Vallandigham) and their antiwar sentiments: "When I read about those Copperhead conventions, those sympathies of treason that I should like to meet them on the field of battle. I would stop firing at the real enemy and turn my rifle upon them."

The Democrats met in Chicago and nominated former Union general George McClellan, fired by Lincoln, as their presidential candidate and Cincinnati congressman George Pendleton as their vice presidential candidate. Vallandigham, who had returned to Ohio in June and was left undisturbed by the Lincoln administration, participated in the Democratic convention and was a main force behind its peace platform (which was not endorsed by McClellan).

Racism was an important theme in the Peace Democrats' opposition to Lincoln's emancipation policy. In a November 5 editorial three days before the 1864 election, the *Cleveland Plain Dealer* had expressed widely held views of the Peace Democrats:

> *Do you want four more years of war?*
> *Vote for Lincoln.*
> *Do you want the Constitution utterly destroyed?*
> *Vote for Lincoln*
> *Do you want the degraded Negroes made your social and political equal?*
> *Vote for Lincoln*
> *Do you want to be arrested and confined in loathsome dungeons without*
> *   process of law and without hope?*
> *Vote for Lincoln*

Meanwhile, Lincoln faced opposition from two prominent Republicans. First, former Ohio governor and senator and Lincoln's treasury secretary Salmon Chase saw himself as the better presidential candidate. According to historian Doris Kearns Goodwin:

Chase certainly believed that he was a much bigger man than Lincoln. As treasury secretary, he had started playing a double game, serving his president while maneuvering to replace him as the party's nominee in 1864. His aims were not unrealistic, given his popularity with the party's liberal base.…Using his superb oratorical skills to set himself apart from the president, Chase had ventured out on his own that October [1863], stumping in Ohio and Indiana before adoring crowds while ostensibly going home to vote in the elections in Columbus.

Frederick Douglass, among other radicals, expressed concern about Lincoln's war policies and his commitment to truly ending slavery. Chase was seen as more committed to ending slavery. A letter (called the "Pomeroy Circular") sent by Chase's supporters (including Ohio senator John Sherman and Ohio congressman James Garfield) in February 1864 raised the possibility of replacing Lincoln as the party's presidential candidate. However, Chase disowned it when he failed to win wider support, and he then backed the candidacy of Lincoln.

On May 31, 1864, a few hundred critics of Lincoln's war policies met in Cleveland to form a new Radical Democratic Party. Its platform included the abolition of slavery by Constitutional amendment and equality before the law for the freed slaves. It nominated as a second alternative to Lincoln for its presidential candidate John C. Frémont. As noted earlier, Frémont had been the Republican Party's first presidential candidate in the 1856 election shortly after it was formed but was defeated by James Buchanan.

Frémont was known as the "Pathfinder" for his explorations in the West that promoted Manifest Destiny and American control of the continent. He also gained national attention for his role in the American seizure of California in 1846. After California became a state following its acquisition after the Mexican-American War, Frémont served as one of its first U.S. senators in 1850–51.

With the outbreak of the Civil War, President Lincoln named Frémont the commander of the Army of the West with the mission of controlling the key border state of Missouri for the Union against strong Confederate forces. Without consulting Lincoln, on August 30, 1861, Frémont issued a proclamation imposing martial law in the state and also emancipating the slaves of rebels. Fearful of alienating the border states where slavery remained legal, Lincoln revoked Frémont's proclamation and eventually removed him from command in the fall.

However, in March 1862, Lincoln restored Frémont to a command, this time of Union forces in Western Virginia and Eastern Kentucky and Tennessee. In June 1862, Frémont engaged Confederate general Stonewall Jackson in two battles in the Shenandoah Valley but failed to defeat him. When he was once again without a military command after that, Frémont resigned from the army in June 1864.

When Frémont accepted the presidential nomination of the Radicals who met in Cleveland, Henry Raymond, editor of the *New York Times* and chairman of the Republican Party, "[c]alled the whole thing 'simply a flank movement against the Administration' that had no hold on public confidence or public sympathy. He called Frémont a 'lost leader.' Stamped by his nomination unmistakably as a political adventurer of the most dangerous sort—buying revenge or success at the price of liberty, striking a 'basic alliance' with the peace Democrats and the haters of equal rights."

While Frémont initially accepted the nomination of this rump group of Radicals who met in Cleveland, in September he withdrew his candidacy, while still remaining critical of Lincoln.

Lincoln became the candidate of the National Union Party with Tennessee Democratic senator Andrew Johnson, the military governor of Tennessee, as his running mate. In September, Lincoln's election fortunes changed when Sherman finally captured Atlanta, giving Northerners the prospect of eventual victory. Union military success was reinforced in October by Philip Sheridan's victories in the Shenandoah Valley.

While some soldiers got furloughs to allow them to vote at home and others voted in camp, nineteen Union states changed their election laws to allow for absentee voting. About 150,000 Union soldiers voted by absentee ballot, with 78 percent voting for Lincoln. Joseph Glatthaar argued:

> *A fresh outlook on the war was just one change that resulted from the presidential election. Lincoln, too, had taken a new image in the eyes of the troops. The man who originally won the presidency with less than 40 percent of the popular vote and had retained it four years later with a 55 percent majority gradually became the symbol of the cause for which he and the troops had battled so very hard to attain. Through good times and bad, Lincoln had stood like a tower of strength, refusing to bend when it came to the cause. His contributions to the war were so important that Sherman's army, with very few exceptions, viewed his election as absolutely essential in the fight to restore the Union and abolish slavery. In the minds of the men, Lincoln had come to represent the struggle to preserve the Union.*

Lincoln was easily reelected with 55.1 percent of the popular vote and 212 electoral votes to only 21 for McClellan. In Ohio, Lincoln defeated McClellan with 56.4 percent of the popular vote and around 80 percent of the Union soldiers' vote. Lincoln carried Cuyahoga County by 3,200 votes and the city of Cleveland by 1,416 votes.

MILITARY HISTORY

Ohio Troops and Generals

During the Civil War, Ohio provided 310,646 troops to the Union's military forces (third only to New York and Pennsylvania) and 230 regiments to the Union army; 35,475 Ohio members of the Union forces lost their lives. Cuyahoga County provided more than 9,000 soldiers and sailors, 1,700 of whom died. Many served in the military units most identified with Cleveland and Cuyahoga County: eight volunteer infantry regiments (the 1st, 7th, 8th, 23rd, 37th, 41st, 103rd and 124th), one cavalry regiment (2nd) and a light artillery battery (1st), which will be profiled next. Ohio Civil War historian James Bissland noted:

> *The fighting in the Western Theater was done largely by Western troops, most of them farmers with calloused hands, from Ohio, Indiana, Illinois, and nearby. They were rough men used to dealing with setbacks and deprivations that trying to make a living from the soil can throw at people.... Inured to hardship and hard times, Western soldiers were endowed with a tremendous capacity to absorb punishment and dish it out with interest.... Troops in the Western Theater tramped thousands of miles with few comforts, persevering despite heat, cold, hunger, and a stubborn foe, to score victory after victory. Ohioans shared their "Westerness" with other Western states, of course. Combined with their numbers and their leaders, Ohioans provided enough force to turn enough turning points to win the war.*

Bissland further described the importance of Ohio's troops in many Union battles in the war:

> *While Ohioans were never a majority at any major battle, they so often formed a substantial minority—[o]ften the largest among the states represented—that it is hard to imagine many Union victories without*

*them.….About fourteen thousand Ohioans participated in Sherman's March
to the Sea. About a fourth of the forces crushing Hood at Nashville were Ohio
infantrymen and artillerymen. By the end of the war, more troops from Ohio
than any other state had spent time in western Virginia protecting loyalists as
they carved a free state of West Virginia out of the Old Dominion. Ohioans
participated, though in smaller numbers, in almost every Eastern Theater
campaign, with several regiments in the thick of the fighting at Antietam and
Gettysburg, and, later, Sheridan's Shenandoah Valley Campaign, as well as
Grant's Overland, Petersburg, and Appomattox campaigns.*

Many of these Ohio regiments served in the Union armies led by the three
Union military heroes most important in defeating the Confederacy: Ulysses
S. Grant, William Tecumseh Sherman and Phil Sheridan. All had Ohio
roots. Grant was born in Point Pleasant, Ohio, and grew up in Georgetown,
Ohio, although he became more associated with Illinois when he wasn't
based elsewhere in the army. When Sherman's father died, he was adopted
by Thomas Ewing, head of a politically important family in Lancaster,
Ohio. Ewing was elected a U.S. senator for one term (1830–36) and served
temporarily in 1850–51. He served Presidents Taylor and Fillmore as the
first secretary of the interior. Sherman married Ellen, his adopted father's
daughter. Three of Ewing's other sons (Thomas, Hugh and Charles) were
Union generals in the Civil War. Sheridan's family emigrated from Ireland,
and Sheridan eventually settled in Somerset, Ohio. All three attended the
U.S. Military Academy at West Point.

In addition to these three most well-known Union military heroes, Ohio
had numerous other Union generals, both successful and not.

Born in Clyde, James Birdseye McPherson graduated first in his class
(which included Philip Sheridan) at the U.S. Military Academy in 1853. At
the beginning of the Civil War, he became a staff officer and was attached
to Ulysses Grant's Army of the Tennessee. In October 1862, he became
a major general. In March 1864, McPherson became commander of the
Army of the Tennessee as Sherman began the campaign to capture Atlanta.
At the Battle of Atlanta on July 22, 1864, McPherson was killed. He was
the second-highest-ranking Union officer and the best-known Union army
commander killed in the Civil War.

Jacob Dolson Cox was a graduate of Oberlin College and before the Civil
War was an educator and lawyer. He helped to organize the Republican Party
in Ohio and was a state legislator. Cox led an Ohio brigade in McClellan's
1862 campaign to secure (West) Virginia for the Union. In September, he

led Ninth Corps troops at the Battles of South Mountain and Antietam. He distinguished himself in the Atlanta, Franklin-Nashville and Carolinas Campaigns in 1864–65. He was Ohio's first postwar governor and served as President Ulysses Grant's first secretary of the interior, promoting civil service reform. Cox broke with Grant and organized Liberal Republicans who unsuccessfully opposed Grant in the 1872 election. He served a single term in Congress (1877–79). He became dean of the University of Cincinnati Law School and later president of the university. He also wrote five books on the Civil War.

Born in New Rumley, George Armstrong Custer graduated last in his class in 1861 at the U.S. Military Academy. Nevertheless, he had a phenomenal rise in the Civil War, becoming the youngest general in the Union army. He played an important role at Gettysburg, in Sheridan's Shenandoah Valley Campaign and in Sheridan's pursuit of Lee that ended in the latter's surrender at Appomattox Court House. After the war, Custer served in the West until his defeat and death on June 25, 1876, at the infamous Battle of the Little Bighorn in Montana.

Born in Taylorsville, George Crook was a career military officer. He was appointed commander of the 36th Ohio Volunteer Infantry (OVI), which first served in western Virginia. Leading a brigade, Crook fought at the Battles of South Mountain and Antietam. He then went west to the Army of the Cumberland and fought at the Battle of Chickamauga. Returning to the East, Crook led an expedition to Southwest Virginia in the spring of 1864. He then served in the Shenandoah Valley Campaign. In February 1865, Crook was captured in a surprise Confederate raid but was exchanged a month later. He finished the Civil War commanding cavalry in the Appomattox Campaign. Crook served in the postwar West, fighting native tribes as well as befriending them.

Irvin McDowell was born in Franklinton and was a career military officer. He became an advisor to Ohio governor Salmon Chase. Appointed to command Union forces in Washington City, McDowell's forces were defeated at the first Battle of Bull Run on July 21, 1861. Nevertheless, McDowell became a corps commander in the Army of the Potomac. His command fought in the Union defeat at the Second Battle of Bull Run. McDowell's actions in both battles were investigated, but he was cleared. Nevertheless, that effectively ended his participation in the Civil War.

A career military officer, Don Carlos Buell was born near Marietta. He first served under McClellan and then succeeded Sherman as head of the Army of the Ohio. Buell's army arrived on April 6, 1862, to help Grant's

Army of the Tennessee defeat the Confederates at Shiloh. On October 8, 1862, Buell's army at the Battle of Perrysville caused the Confederates to withdraw from Kentucky. However, Buell's dilatory actions were investigated by a military commission led by General Lew Wallace. After that, Buell refused a new command and resigned from the army.

Born in Delaware County, William Rosecrans went to the U.S. Military Academy and served in the prewar army until 1854, when he resigned to go into business. Rosecrans briefly commanded the 23rd OVI and then served under McClellan in (West) Virginia in 1861, but he was replaced in 1862 by John C. Frémont. Rosecrans (known as "Old Rosy") was assigned to the West and took command of the Union Army of the Mississippi. His actions at the 1862 Battles of Iuka and Corinth were controversial. In October 1862, Rosecrans was appointed commander of the Army of the Cumberland. At the battle of Stone's River, Tennessee, from December 31, 1862, to January 1, 1863, he repulsed Braxton Bragg's Confederate Army of Tennessee. In the summer of 1863, Rosecrans's Tullahoma Campaign forced Bragg's army from Chattanooga. However, Rosecrans's army was defeated at the Battle of Chickamauga on September 19–20 (the only major defeat of Union armies in the West). He retreated to Chattanooga, where his army was besieged by Bragg. U.S. Grant arrived on October 23 to take command and relieved Rosecrans of command of the Army of the Cumberland. Rosecrans served in Missouri in 1864. After the war, he eventually moved to California. He served two terms in Congress (1880–84). Known for his temper and his devotion to Catholicism, Rosecrans became involved in disputes with Presidents Ulysses Grant and James Garfield.

West Virginia

After Virginia seceded from the Union, a movement began in its more pro-Union mountainous region to secede from Virginia. Union forces, which included several Ohio regiments, soon crossed the Ohio River into the area to drive out the Confederates. They first defeated Confederates at Philippi on June 3, 1861. Then, commanded by General George McClellan, they again defeated Confederates at the Battle of Rich Mountain on July 11, 1861. This victory made McClellan a Northern military hero. Lincoln recalled him after the Union defeat at the first Battle of Bull Run. McClellan arrived in Washington City on November 26 and organized the Army of the Potomac, which he then first commanded. In (West) Virginia, a secessionist convention met beginning also on November 26 that would result in fifty western counties seceding from the Confederacy. The new state of West Virginia was admitted to the Union on June 20, 1863. In 1861, Generals William Rosecrans and Jacob Dolson Cox also commanded Union troops in western Virginia. General Robert E. Lee commanded the Confederate forces. Fighting in West Virginia would continue during the rest of the war, with Union forces largely controlling the region.

Camp Cleveland

As men in Northern Ohio answered President Lincoln's call for volunteers to fight the rebellion, several training camps were established in Cleveland, according to Phyllis Anne Flower:

> The conditions in the camps were poor during the early months of the war as it was necessary to quarter soldiers before adequate preparations were made. The men had to put up with rude and scant accommodations. The hastily constructed barracks had bunks arranged along narrow aisles and gave the impression of shelves in an apple bin. The women in Cleveland were moved by reports of such poor conditions to solicit bedding and mattresses for the camps.

Among these camps was Camp Cleveland, a thirty-five-and-a-half-acre site in what was then called University Heights and later Lincoln Heights (today it's called Tremont). It opened in July 1862. It comprised barracks for the troops, an arsenal, a guardhouse, a chapel and a military hospital.

Dale Thomas described the departure of the 103rd infantry regiment with hundreds of recruits from Cuyahoga County from Camp Cleveland in September 1862:

> With only a week left at Camp Cleveland, Colonel James Casement, commander of the 103rd OVI, allowed picnics for the ten companies of his regiment.…The company picnics had been combined into one large goodbye party. In the middle of the parade ground, tables were placed in a square and "loaded with good things-turkeys, chickens, roast beef, cold tongue, ham, biscuit and butter, pickles, jellies, pie…." After the soldiers stuffed themselves, they removed the tables, and "dancing to inspiring music of the two brass bands present, was commenced and kept up for two to three

hours."...An hour before sunset, the men marched in formation, and they "will ever remember the day with pleasure."...On September 3 [1862], the soldiers of the 103rd Infantry received their bounties before departing at 6:00 a.m. for the Union Depot in Cleveland. Shield's Battery fired a captured Rebel cannon, and Clark's Forest City Band marched out of camp with the regiment. "Superior Street was full of curious lookers-on and friends of the boys. [It was] the wildest scene we have witnessed since the departure of our first volunteers—the Cleveland Grays." A very large number of people, mostly relatives and friends of the departing soldiers were at the depot to say farewell, and there were many tearful partings.

Over the course of the war, 15,230 men would pass through Camp Cleveland (about 5 percent of Ohio's total of Union enlistments during the war). Life in the Union army for these soldiers will be described. The hospital treated more than 3,000 sick and wounded soldiers.

During the course of the war, women became critical to the care of wounded soldiers. In June 1861, Dorothea Dix was named the first superintendent of U.S. Army nurses. She was overshadowed by Clara Barton, who served at several major battles in the eastern theater of war. Barton became the postwar first president of the American Red Cross.

While serving in the Sea Islands of South Carolina in 1863, helping liberated slaves, Barton met Colonel John J. Elwell, a doctor, lawyer and professor from Cleveland. He was serving as the Union quartermaster on Port Royal Island. Barton nursed him back to health from yellow fever. Despite Elwell's marriage, they became intimate friends. Barton and Elwell left to witness the Union attacks on the Confederate fortifications defending Charleston. This included the famous assault on July 18, 1863, on Battery Wagner by the African American 54th Massachusetts infantry regiment, led

Camp Cleveland Hospital. *Courtesy of Chris Roy.*

Union nurse Clara Barton, 1865. *Courtesy of Library of Congress.*

by Colonel Robert Shaw. Witnessing the slaughter of the regiment, Elwell raced toward them and was shot from his horse. Clara came to his rescue. She stayed to nurse Union casualties, while Elwell returned to Hilton Head. Later that year, she rejoined him there. Elwell was breveted four times for bravery during the war. They met again after the war when Barton lectured in Cleveland. They remained friends and corresponded. Upon his death in 1900, Barton wrote a testimonial for Elwell.

Another nursing heroine to Union soldiers was "Mother" Mary Bickerdyke, born in Mount Vernon, Ohio. She traveled with Union armies throughout the war, establishing more than three hundred field hospitals. She was present at nineteen major battles and accompanied Sherman's armies during the Atlanta Campaign and the March to the Sea. At the Grand Review of the Armies in Washington City in May 1865, Bickerdyke rode at the head of Sherman's Fifteenth Corps. After the war, she became an attorney and helped secure pensions for veterans and female nurses.

Soldiers would generally come to Camp Cleveland after arriving in Cleveland at the Union Depot train station. A "Secesh" cannon captured in (West) Virginia by the Cleveland Light Artillery was fired to celebrate Union victories. Before Camp Cleveland was closed in July 1865, more than eleven thousand troops were paid and discharged (mustered out) there. In October 2003, an Ohio historical marker was erected in Tremont to commemorate Camp Cleveland.

Life in the Union Army

From soldiers' letters, noted Civil War historian James McPherson examined the several reasons that citizen-soldiers fought and died for the Union. High among them was love of their country and a sense of duty to serve. This was more difficult for married soldiers, who received letters from their wives and families urging them to return home. McPherson cited this example as typical:

"It is for the future welfare of your selfe and children, that causes me to be separated from you," wrote a lieutenant in the 41ˢᵗ Ohio to his wife. "If you esteem me with a true womans love you will not ask me to disgrace myself by deserting the flag of our Union....Remember that however much I would like to be at home, to enjoy the sweet comforts of life, the society of a dear wife, and children, yet what is life worth, without a government under which it can be enjoyed....I will again return to you as soon as honor alone will permit."

Mail was very important both to the soldiers in the field and their families and relatives back home:

Home circumstances has an enormous influence on morale. A soldier who was confident that his loved ones were healthy, adequately provided with food, clothing and shelter, well treated by relatives and neighbors, constant in their affections and optimistic in their outlook was better satisfied with his lot than one whose family conditions were a source of anxiety. Letters bringing any sort of bad news from home were apt to be upsetting, and if told of want, sickness, neglect or persecution by kinfolk, unfriendlessness of neighbors, or indicated a weakness of marital bonds, they might lead to complete demoralization and desertion.

German American Clevelander George Elliot Sohl of the 124ᵗʰ OVI received this message from his wife, Emaline, after she heard her preacher talk about the dangers of soldiers straying from their marital vows when she hoped that he "wouldn't lose your character." Sohl responded, "I will do my best to come home a better man then [*sic*] when I left." He described the joy of receiving mail while stationed in Franklin, Tennessee, in March 1863: "You cannot tell how much good it did me to hear from home once more." The Union military postal system was generally good, although letters from home were often delayed while units were on the march or engaged in combat. Soldiers often sent their pay home in the mail. They also had their photos taken and sent home by mail.

During the winter of 1862–63, Joseph Briggs, a worker in Cleveland's only federal postal office (located on Public Square), was concerned about women (including those with husbands and sons and friends in the Union army) having to come there in the wintry weather to send or pick up mail (unless they were able to hire private carriers). Briggs proposed an innovative experiment: to deliver the mail. It was approved by the Cleveland postmaster (who was also the publisher of the *Cleveland Leader* newspaper) and then the U.S. postmaster general. First, the mail was sent to grocery stores, and later it began to be delivered to specific addresses. On March 3, 1863, this experiment was authorized by Congress to be expanded to fifty-two cities. Briggs was first appointed as the special agent to implement this system, and later he became its national superintendent. Briggs also helped design the first uniform for mail carriers.

Despite the material advantages enjoyed by the North and its supplies to the Union armies, its soldiers did suffer. First, there was disease. More than twice as many Union soldiers died of disease compared to combat deaths. For example, George Lewis, major of Company B of the 124th OVI, wrote about this problem in its encampment in Tennessee in August 1863: "[M]en were afflicted with that terrible disease, that with the aid of the government and its surgeons, has slain its thousands, known as camp; or chronic diarrhoea." Poor sanitation in camps and contaminated water were two of the major causes of this disease. Lewis complained of poor conditions in the field hospitals, arguing for furloughs for sick soldiers, who could better recover at their homes.

Soldiers often competed for water with their horses. An example of the problem of poor water on the march was that of the 103rd OVI in Kentucky in 1862, as told by a soldier, quoted by William Stark:

> *Drinking water was scarce because of the lack of rain. The 103rd Regiment camped near a "foul and stagnant" pond of green, scummy water called Snow's Pond. The water was too filthy to be a duck pond and unfit for animals to drink….Frank Campbell of Company G repulsively chronicled that "the water where we were is very Poor it is nothing but pond water & when it begins to boil there will be a green skum rise on it two or three times I believe if we don't get where there is better water we wil all be sick."*

In addition to these factors, Bell Irvin Wiley also cited enlistment of "unfit" men, lack of immunization against smallpox, poor diet at times, incompetent medical staff and inadequate hospitalization facilities.

Many soldiers in training camps initially suffered from the measles. In its training camp south of Louisville in December 1861, just one case led to an epidemic within the 41st OVI, requiring the hospitalization of more than one hundred recruits. Its historians, Kimberly and Holloway, noted:

At the same time typhoid fever prevailed to an alarming extent, and our cases of measles were no sooner on their feet than a large proportion of them came down with that disease. Malaria, camp diarrhea and jaundice abounded. Including the convalescents there were at one time 300 men off duty.

A sad individual case was that of Clevelander Harvey Loomis. He enlisted in the 103rd OVI in Cleveland on November 23, 1863; joined the regiment in Tennessee on January 5, 1864; contracted measles and was hospitalized in Knoxville on January 14; and died on January 19, 1864. An officer of his company lamented:

Thus, another one of America's sons have laid their lives on the altar of our country and fallen a victim to disease again those rebelling against the government have to answer for the life of that youthful lad and soldier.

On the march, troops often suffered hardship. For example, the 103rd OVI was part of General Ambrose Burnside's army pursuing General James Longstreet's retreating Confederate force after its failed attack on Knoxville, Tennessee, in December 1863, as Thomas noted:

[They] *marched dripping wet in the cold weather along muddy roads. According to Captain Hayes, "the troops were in no condition to march. Half of them were no more than half clad, and all were nearly destitute of shoes. Provisions were limited, and the Commissary could furnish only half rations at most."*

Perhaps the most difficult march by a Union army during the war was William Tecumseh Sherman's Carolinas Campaign of 1865 following his March to the Sea and the capture of Savannah. His army had to contend with swamps, prolonged rain and mud that made it so hard to march that, according to Joseph Glatthaar,

shoes were the largest clothing problem in Sherman's army. The shoe shortage first appeared during the Savannah campaign, and the army did get a supply at the coast, but those who received them found that the soles fell off after brief usage and there were not enough for everyone in need....By the time the army reached Goldsboro [North Carolina], *there were nearly 4,000 barefoot in the Seventeenth Corps alone....Some shoeless men tied gunnysacks or rawhide strips around their feet to protect them from the cold.*

Civil War soldiers carried heavy packs in addition to their weapons. Cleveland soldier John Rieley described in a March 20, 1864 letter what he was carrying in his knapsack upon marching out of Knoxville: two big blankets, four shirts, five pairs of socks, an overcoat, one jacket and a lot of small trinkets, a haversack full of grub, a canteen and a coffeepot. John Billings also described marching conditions in bad weather that Union soldiers endured:

The army on the march in a rainstorm presented some aspects not seen in fair weather. As soon as it began to rain or just before, each man would remove his rubber blanket from his roll or knapsack, and put it over his shoulders, tying it in front. Some men used their shelter tent instead—a very poor substitute, however. But there was no fun in the marching business in the rain. It might settle the dust. It certainly settled everything else. An order to go into camp while the rain was in progress was not much of an improvement, for the ground was wet, fence-rails were wet, one's woolen blanket was likely also to be wet, hardtack in the haversack wet—in fact, nothing so abundant and out of place as water.

Another problem was poor diet. Soldiers relied heavily on hardtack and salted meat for their meals. Hardtack often presented one of these three problems, as Billings continued:

First, they may have been so hard that they could not be bitten; it then required a very strong blow of the fist to break them....The second condition was when they were mouldy or wet, as sometimes happened, and should not have been given to the soldiers. I think this condition was often due to their having been boxed up too soon after baking. It certainly was frequently due to exposure to the weather....The third condition was when from storage they had become infested with maggots and weevils. These weevils were, in my experience, more abundant than the maggots. They were a little slim, brown bug an eighth of an inch in length, and were great bores on a small scale, having the ability to completely riddle the hardtack. I believe that they never interfered with the hardest variety. When the bread was mouldy or moist, it was thrown away and made good at the next drawing, so that the men were not the losers; but in the case of being infested with the weevils, they had to stand it as a rule; for the biscuits had to be pretty thoroughly alive, and well covered with the webs which these creatures left, to insure condemnation.

Another problem, according to Billings, was storing rations:

> [A] *raw recruit just arrived would take it up in a paper, and stow it away in that well known receptacle for all eatables, the soldier's haversack, only to find it part of a general mixture of hardtack, salt, pork, pepper, knife, fork, spoon, sugar, and coffee by the time the next halt was made. A recruit of longer standing, who had been through this experience and had begun to feel his wisdom-teeth coming, would take his up in a bag made of scrap of rubber blanket or a* poncho; *but after a few days carrying the rubber would peel off or the paint of the* poncho *would rub off from contact with the greasy pork or boiled meat ration which was its travelling companion, and make a black, dirty mess, besides leaving the coffee-bag unfit for further use.*

A staple of the army diet was the bean:

> *The bean ration was an important factor in the sustenance of the army, and no edible, I think, was so thoroughly appreciated. Company cooks stewed them with pork, and when the pork was good and the stew or soup was well done and not burned—a rare combination of circumstances—they were quite palatable in this way.*

Vegetables were often not a staple. Instead:

> *Occasionally, a ration of what was known as desiccated vegetables was dealt out. This consisted of a small piece per man, an ounce in weight and two or three inches cube of a sheet or block of vegetables, which had been prepared, and apparently* kiln-dried, *as sanitary* fodder *for soldiers.... In brief, this coarse vegetable compound could with much more propriety have been put before Southern swine than Northern soldiers. "Desecrated vegetables" was the more appropriate name which the men quite generally applied to this preparation of husks.*

Therefore, when actual vegetables were available, soldiers celebrated. After the capture of Atlanta, Lewis of the 124th OVI wrote:

> *We had not been in camp many days before we were astonished by the news that the Sanitary Commission, a patriotic organization of the loyal citizens of the north (whose ramifications penetrated to every city, village,*

hamlet and farm of the loyal states), had sent us a train load of Irish potatoes. This may seem a small matter to take note of after so many years and read to you, who in all your lives have never known the want of anything to eat your appetites might crave, but what do you say to a lot of men that from January 1ˢᵗ, 1863, to September, 1864, had not feasted, even with their eyes, on a potato? If you could, at your home, surrounded with all the delicacies of the culinary art, be deprived of the common potato for eighteen months, you could then appreciate our situation. The cheers and shouting that went up, mid-afternoon, when the commissary department sent word to the regiments it had potatoes to issue, were enough to make you think the news of some great victory had been communicated to us. And when the stream of potatoes began to be diverted and divided to the companies and messes, it was too comical for anything, those great bronzed and weather-beaten soldiers, running around with their hands full of potatoes, and to see the fires lighted at that time of day, and the little kettles, or pails rather, filled and brimming full of potatoes; then when cooled to see the feasting-potatoes served with salt. I suppose you would demand nice Jersey butter, but salt was good enough for us. And this is not all I have to say of that commission organized from the loyal citizens of the north. It brought us by carload, pickled cabbage and onions; and how refreshing they were to us that had not tasted vegetable food for eighteen long months. I do not believe there is an old veteran alive to-day that does not bless from the bottom of his heart, that greatest and most magnificent of charities ever organized—the Sanitary Commission.

Homefront Support

The Union troops in the field received the support of citizens back home. In Cleveland and its surrounding communities, there was no more important group than the women of the Soldiers' Aid Society and those who worked in the U.S. Sanitary Commission, according to Bell Irvin Wiley:

The United States Sanitary Commission was far and away the most outstanding of voluntary benevolent organizations…it coordinated and turned into useful channels the activities of hundreds of small groups, raised millions of dollars, purchased and distributed vast amounts of food, clothing, medicines and supplies, provided scores of nurses and doctors at critical times, and equipped, staffed, and put into operation hospital boats, trains and other numerous facilities. Its agents conducted innumerable inspections, collected valuable data and kept the country informed as to the needs and conditions of the sick and wounded.

Soldiers' Aid Society of Northern Ohio

Soon after President Lincoln's call for volunteers after the Confederates bombarded Fort Sumter in April 1861, the Cleveland branch of the Soldiers' Aid Society (also associated with the U.S. Sanitary Commission) was organized by Rebecca Rouse, as Van Tassel and Vacha described:

On Friday, April 19, the Herald *published a notice addressed to "The patriotic ladies of Cleveland, anxious and ready to take their full share in the exertions and privations, if need be, imposed by the public perils," inviting them to attend a meeting at Chapin's Hall on the corner of Euclid and Public Square on Saturday, April 20 at three o'clock. The following afternoon Euclid Avenue was crowded with carriages carrying ladies, matrons, and young girls; and lines of women wearing bonnets and long coats in muted colors streamed toward the three-story brownstone building that was Chapin's Hall. They climbed the stairways to the third floor, where they emerged into a grand, gas-lit auditorium containing 1,200 upholstered seats. When the hall filled, the noise level dropped as a short, gray-haired woman strode with serious purpose to the podium. Mrs. Benjamin (Rebecca) Rouse was a familiar figure to many of the ladies in the audience who worked with the Protestant Orphanage Society, the Cleveland Ladies Temperance Union, or the Protestant Sunday schools. She wasted no time in getting to the purpose of the meeting, which was to organize the women of Cleveland to raise funds and collect supplies for volunteers and their families. After electing officers and pledging twenty-five cents a month as members of the new Ladies' Aid Society (soon to be called the Soldiers' Aid Society of Northern Ohio), the women divided up into ward visiting committees to see to the needs of the families of soldiers.*

One of its earliest activities was the "blanket raid" shortly after the earliest volunteers arrived at training camps in Cleveland without supplies, including uniforms and bedding. The women roamed the streets of the city collecting blankets for the soldiers. Later raids sought clothing and vegetables. It

Soldiers' Aid Society. *Courtesy of Chris Roy.*

The Northern Ohio Soldiers' Aid Society, Sanitary Commission and Hospital Service Corps (Soldiers' and Sailors' Monument, Cleveland, Ohio). *Photo by Kay L. Martin.*

supported Union soldiers and their families throughout the war, including at the Soldiers' Home, which it built in 1863. In 1864, it organized a Sanitary Fair in Cleveland to help finance its activities.

Ten leaders from the society are commemorated in Cleveland's Soldiers' and Sailors' Monument, including Rebecca Rouse.

Rouse and her husband arrived in Cleveland in 1830 from New York. In 1842, she founded and was president of the Martha Washington & Orcas Society, which created the Protestant Orphan Asylum, which she directed. In 1850, she helped organize the Cleveland Ladies Temperance Union. Rebecca Rouse served as the president of the Cleveland Soldiers' Aid Society throughout the war.

Soldiers' Home

In 1863, the Soldiers' Aid Society engaged in a major project: the building of a Soldiers' Home by the Lakeside Depot. It was designed to serve meals and accommodate wounded soldiers in transit, as noted by Phyllis Anne Flower. It opened in December:

> *All physical equipment for the rooms was obtained by public solicitation. It was not an unusual sight to see buggies and wagons piled high with cots, bed-clothes, mattresses, pails, brooms, and staple foods arrive at the depot with contributions from all parts of the county.*

Soldiers' Home: For the Relief of Union Soldiers at Cleveland. *Courtesy of Chris Roy.*

By war's end, it had provided shelter to more than fifty-seven thousand Union soldiers and served more than 111,000 meals. The home continued its work for several years after the close of the war and aided considerably in caring for itinerant soldiers on their way home.

1864 Northern Ohio Sanitary Fair

In September 1863, Rebecca Rouse and the officers of the Soldiers' Aid Society of Northern Ohio visited a fair organized in Chicago by their counterparts. In November, they announced that they were planning for a similar event in Cleveland. A building in the shape of a Greek cross was constructed on Public Square around the Perry Monument, as described by Flower:

> *The exhibits, which were entirely donated, as well as the attendance more than realized all expectations. People thronged the streets, stores, exhibit halls, and railroad depots. The railways were cooperative in charging only half-fare for passengers holding fair tickets and in carrying donations to the fair free of freight charges.*

On Washington's Birthday, February 22, 1864, the Sanitary Fair opened, and a dinner was held at the Weddell House hotel celebrating the event. Major General James Garfield, then a congressman, delivered a keynote address paying homage to the women and children of the homefront. The fair closed on March 10 and was a financial success, raising $78,000. According to David Van Tassel and John Vacha:

> [The] *financial and spiritual uplift provided by the fair sustained the Soldiers' Aid Society of Northern Ohio to the end of the war more than a year later. They began with a capital of two dollars and closed with a cash statement of $170,000 in 1869. From a neighborhood sewing circle, it grew into a network of 25 branch organizations. It built and sponsored a Soldiers' Home and dispensed hospital stores valued at $1 million. It sent clothing and food to soldiers in the field and gave aid and comfort to their families at home. Even after the end of hostilities, it continued as an employment service and claims agency for returning veterans.*

In one of the more unusual wartime initiatives in Cleveland, members of the Old Stone Church created the "Home for Friendless Strangers." It provided assistance, including medical care, to war refugees.

Military Units

The experience of Cleveland's Civil War volunteer soldiers can be found in letters, diaries, regimental histories and other documents, as will be relied on throughout these sections. Their experience is illustrated in the following military units, which had large numbers of soldiers from Cleveland, as well as elsewhere in Cuyahoga County.

CLEVELAND GRAYS

This local militia was formed in 1837 as a military unit originally called the Cleveland City Guards. In 1838, it became known as the Cleveland Grays from the color of its uniforms. Its motto was *Semper Paratus* ("Always Prepared"). George Vourlojianis described the unit that answered President Lincoln's call for volunteers:

> *The militia company that left Cleveland on that April* [18] *afternoon in 1861* [for Camp Jackson in Columbus] *was in many ways different from that organized by Timothy Ingraham twenty-four years before. Their average age was now only twenty-three. And in order to meet the state's quota of seventy-five men, the Grays opened their ranks for the first time to the general public. In addition to Cleveland's elite, their numbers now included bank clerks, students, tradesmen, railroaders, saloon keepers, and a brewer.*

Phyliss Anne Flower described its departure: "A crowd of fifteen thousand people thronged city streets to cheer and bid farewell to the troops, who left the union depot as Leland's band played 'Yankee Doodle' and 'The Girl I Left Behind Me.'" The Cleveland Bible Society gave each soldier a Bible.

Two companies of the 84th Ohio Volunteer Infantry (OVI) organized in June 1861 were members of the Cleveland Grays. It primarily served guard duty in Virginia and was mustered out in Cleveland on September 20, 1862. Then, two companies of the 29th Ohio National Guard (redesignated the 150th OVI and incorporated into the Union army in May 1864), composed of the Grays, were sent to defend Washington City. It was there when

Cleveland Grays. *Courtesy of Chris Roy.*

General Jubal Early's Confederate army threatened the capital on July 11–12, 1864. The 150th OVI was then mustered out and arrived in Cleveland on August 14, where it was greeted by welcoming crowds.

Among its ranks were several who would later become prominent in Cleveland and Ohio: Marcus Hanna, businessman and U.S. senator; Allan Brinsmade, U.S. senator; George Nash, Ohio Supreme Court justice; and Herman Chapin and Perry Payne, mayors of Cleveland. The last military service of some of the Grays was to serve in the honor guard when President Lincoln's body arrived in Cleveland on April 28, 1865. According to George Vourlojianis:

> *In Cleveland, not only service in general but service with the Grays in particular could do nothing but enhance one's electoral appeal. The returned veterans formed a business and commercial network that provided the organization and its members with a variety of goods and services. Because of their Civil War service, the Grays redefined themselves as part of a new economic and political elite.*

HIBERNIAN GUARDS

The Irish were the second-largest group of European immigrants (the Germans being the largest) to come to Cleveland. They came to work on building the Ohio and Erie Canal. During the famine of the late 1840s, many of the Famine Irish immigrated to Cleveland, where they found work on the docks and as laborers. These immigrants initially settled in an area just west of the Cuyahoga River that became known as Irishtown Bend, part of a larger Irish settlement known as the "Angle." In 1850, 46 percent of Cleveland's population was foreign-born. The Irish counted for 2,200 out of the city's population of around 17,000. Because of their Roman Catholic religion that most adhered to, the Irish encountered considerable discrimination. A Nativist political party—the Know Nothings—arose based largely on opposition to the Catholic immigrants. Edwin Cowles, editor of the *Cleveland Leader* newspaper, was anti-Catholic and headed the Cleveland chapter of the anti-Catholic Order of the American Union.

During the Civil War, an estimated 150,000 Irish Americans served in the Union army. Many were recruited as soon as they landed in the eastern seaports. While some joined for the pay, others had patriotic reasons for joining the army. A Cleveland example was Frank Rieley, the son of Irish emigrants, who enlisted at age nineteen in Company I, 103rd OVI. In letters to his mother, Margaret, he wrote, "I think it is the duty of at least one out of each family to go and fight for his country." His brother John also served in the 19th Ohio Battery. Rieley was captured briefly by John Hunt Morgan's cavalry in Lexington, Kentucky, in November 1862 but escaped. Rieley later transferred to the cavalry and had a horse shot out from under him in Tennessee. From Murfreesboro, Tennessee, on February 11, 1863, Frank wrote to his mother, "I wish for a Cleveland paper. It would be like an old friend."

The most famous Irish unit in the Army of the Potomac was the Irish Brigade, composed of several eastern regiments. Cleveland's example was the Hibernian Guards. Comprising Irish Americans, it was formed as a militia unit in 1847. With the beginning of the Civil War, it first served in the three-month 1st OVI. It then enlisted for three years and served in the 8th OVI. The Hibernian Guards have been remembered by contemporary Civil War reenactors. Their "colonel" said of thanks by attendees of an annual St. Patrick's Day parade in Cleveland, "I didn't take that for me.…I took it for the old boys." Every recent August, a Civil War reenactment is held at the Hale Farm & Village, located south of Cleveland, which is part of the Western Reserve Historical Society.

Thomas Francis Galwey, one of the members of the Hibernian Guards, kept a diary of his service in the 8th OVI, and it provides considerable insight into the experience of Cleveland's Civil War soldiers. Galwey's Irish family immigrated to the United States from London and eventually settled on a farm in Cleveland.

7TH OVI

The 7th OVI was the first regiment raised in Cleveland (April 1861). The regiment was known as "the Roosters" for its battle cry of crowing. It had three companies solely composed of men from Cleveland. Company C was composed of students who came from Oberlin and was commanded by Giles Shurtleff. The war fever was rampant at Oberlin College, where the quick formation of a company among the boys was matched by the organization of a "Florence Nightingale Association" by the girls.

On August 26, 1861, the 7th OVI was routed by Confederates at the Battle of Cross Lanes in what became West Virginia. Shurtleff was captured along with others from his company, and he spent a year in captivity in various Confederate prisons before he was exchanged. Company K was composed solely of German Americans. Of this company's total of 150 during the war, 27 were killed and 30 wounded in combat.

During its three years of service, this regiment fought in some of the most famous battles and campaigns in the Civil War. In the Eastern Theater, these included the 1862 Shenandoah Valley Campaign against Stonewall Jackson, who was defeated at the first Battle of Kernstown near Winchester. At Cedar Mountain, Virginia, on August 9, 1862, attacking Jackson's force, Colonel William Creighton and Major Orrin Crane were both wounded. Creighton was a printer at the *Cleveland Herald* who had recruited Company A. Crane was a carpenter for a Cleveland shipbuilder.

The regiment suffered badly, with 191 out of 307 killed or wounded. Cleveland's Company A's casualties were 24 out of 30, and Oberlin's Company C saw 18 out of 21. Next came the Battle of Second Manassas.

At Antietam on September 17, 1862 (the bloodiest day of the war), the 7th OVI fought at the Dunker Church and the East Woods against Jackson's force, suffering forty-three casualties out of its one hundred members. Timothy Mieyal noted:

> *As the year 1863 dawned, members of the 7th Ohio could look back on their time of service as an active yet destructive period. Less than one year earlier, the harsh reality of battle and large-scale suffering had been unknown to them. Their participation in seven battles had resulted in the deaths of nearly 100 comrades while total casualties had already exceeded 600. Unfortunately, these casualties continued to accumulate as many of the wounded men never recovered. Only about one-third of the once proud 1,000 men who had been mustered into service in the summer of 1861 remained on New Year's Day*

Left: Lieutenant Colonel Orrin I. Crane of Company A, 7th Ohio Infantry Regiment, in uniform. *Courtesy of Library of Congress.*

Right: Colonel William R. Creighton of 7th Ohio Infantry Regiment in uniform, 1861. *Courtesy of Library of Congress.*

1863. By this time, the 7th Ohio had suffered as much for the cause as almost any other Union regiment. Throughout the coming year, they would tolerate much of the same as participation in the great campaigns of the war continued to diminish their rapidly thinning ranks.

At the Battle of Chancellorsville in May 1863, the regiment had only four hundred fit for duty and suffered another one hundred casualties as Joseph Hooker's army was defeated by Robert E. Lee. At Gettysburg, it defended Culp's Hill on the third day against attacks by the Stonewall Brigade. There is a monument in Gettysburg dedicated to the regiment.

After the battle, the regiment was sent to New York City (August 29– September 7) to help quell the July draft riots, although they had ended by the time the regiment arrived. Many of the rioters were Irish immigrants who had not volunteered to serve in the Union army and were protesting against conscription and also being asked to fight to free slaves who might compete with them for jobs. They were especially angry that the rich could buy their way out of military service by hiring substitutes for $300. The rioting cost many lives, including those of Black residents who were attacked at random.

Following that duty, the 7th OVI left the Army of the Potomac and went west to Chattanooga, where it participated in the lifting of the Confederate siege in November 1864. It fought in the assault in the fog on Lookout Mountain (the "Battle above the Clouds"). It then joined in the pursuit of Braxton Bragg's Army of Tennessee into Northern Georgia. On November 26, the 7th OVI, led by Crane under the command of the brigade now led by Creighton, was ordered to assault Bragg's rearguard at Ringgold Gap. It was held by General Patrick Cleburne, who had blocked Sherman at Missionary Ridge on November 25. First, Crane was killed, followed by Creighton. The casualties of the 7th OVI totaled ninety, including twelve of thirteen commissioned officers. Company C lost fourteen of twenty men. Before being shot, Creighton had saved the life of a wounded Captain George McKay of the 7th OVI. In his battle report, McKay wrote, "Every officer and soldier who marched up the mountainside, toward the ridge, in that charge of Creighton's brigade was a hero." Captain Ernst Krieger was the only officer not killed or wounded, and he took command after Crane's death. He wrote:

> We are stunned by the loss of our colonels. We had fondly hoped that, having passed through so many battles, they would be spared to take us home in the spring. The loss will not be felt by us alone, it will be felt throughout the corps and at home.

Cleveland's civic leaders arranged for the bodies of the two fallen colonels to lie in state at city hall. Their funeral was held on December 8, 1863, at the Old Stone Church next to Public Square, as described by Timothy Mieyal. After the funeral oration:

> The long procession filed out of the church around 1:00 PM and eventually made its way to Erie Street Cemetery where thousands more had gathered. This was to be the temporary resting place until Woodland Cemetery was readied. The military formed in a square around the grave. The pall-bearers advanced forward and deposited both bodies together into their resting place. The Reverend W.A. Fiske led the brief burial service and then three volleys were fired over the graves by soldiers of the 7th Ohio. Then, it was over and slowly and mournfully the vast multitudes turned away and went home.

They are buried side by side at Woodland Cemetery.

Creighton and Crane gravestones, Woodland Cemetery, Cleveland, Ohio. *Photo by Kay L. Martin.*

In 1864, as part of the Army of the Cumberland, the 7th OVI fought in several of the battles in Ohioan William Tecumseh Sherman's Atlanta Campaign. Its three-year enlistments expired before Sherman captured Atlanta. The 7th OVI mustered out in Cleveland July 6–7, 1864; 250 survivors were met at the Cleveland train depot by thousands. Timothy Mieyal concluded:

> *After being honored with their close friends in the 5th Ohio in Cincinnati, the 7th Ohio finally made it home to Cleveland to enjoy a well-deserved celebration in their name. Though other regiments had been formed in Cleveland including the 8th and 41st Infantry and the 2nd Cavalry, the 7th Ohio had always been the city's favorite. On July 4, 1864, a huge celebration took place in downtown Cleveland to commemorate Independence Day and to thank the 7th Ohio for a job well done. The 7th Ohio's reputation for valor extended far beyond the Western Reserve.*

During its service, it lost 10 officers (including its colonels) and 174 other men in combat and 2 officers and 87 soldiers to disease. A total of 610 Clevelanders served in the 7th OVI. This included John D. Rockefeller's younger brother Frank Rockefeller, who was twice wounded.

1st OVI

The 1st OVI enlisted for three months in response to President Lincoln's call for volunteers after the April 12, 1861 attack on Fort Sumter in the harbor of Charleston, South Carolina. Two companies were from Cleveland: Company E comprised members of the Cleveland Grays, where three members were the first German Americans to serve in the army. Company F comprised members of Cleveland's Hibernian Guards. Sent to Washington City, it saw its first fighting on June 17, 1861, at Vienna, Virginia. The Grays, traveling on a train, were ambushed by South Carolina troops and suffered their first casualty, a mortally wounded lieutenant. They then participated in the first battle of Bull Run on July 21, 1861; the 1st OVI was the last unit to cover the Union army's retreat. One of the soldiers from the Grays was mortally wounded. He was buried at Cleveland's Woodland Cemetery. After the 1st OVI was mustered out, many of its members enlisted in the three-year 1st OVI. The Grays returned home on August 3, 1861, and were greeted by welcoming crowds and a dinner honoring their service. The welcoming committee did not so honor the returning Hibernian Guards.

The 1st OVI served in the Western Theater and fought at many major battles, including Shiloh, Stone's River, Chickamauga, Chattanooga (Orchard Knob and Missionary Ridge), Resaca and Kennesaw Mountain. It claimed to be the first Union regiment to scale the crest of Missionary Ridge in the unordered assault of November 25, 1864, that lifted the Siege of Chattanooga, according to Bissland:

> *For the rest of their lives, the attackers of Mission*[ary] *Ridge would argue over who was first to reach the top. Gen. William B. Hazen* [a boyhood friend of James Garfield and the first commander of the 41st OVI] *devoted fifty pages of his memoirs to insisting that it was one of his regiments—the 1st Ohio. Led up the slope by long-legged Lt. Col. E. Bassett Langdon, the Ohioans paused to catch their breath in a sheltered spot just three yards short of the top. Then—according to Hazen—they broke over the crest while other regiments were still climbing. Colonel Langdon was shot through the face.*

The three-year 1st OVI fought in twenty-four western battles and skirmishes. It suffered 527 casualties. Company E had 8 killed and 13 wounded (plus 9 dead from disease). Company F had 11 killed or wounded.

23RD OVI

The 23rd OVI was best known for several of its later famous members. One of its commanders was Rutherford B. Hayes, later governor of Ohio and president of the United States. William McKinley was also to later become a president of the United States. McKinley was both the last president to be a Civil War veteran and the second Ohio U.S. president to be assassinated. Others in this regiment included Stanley Matthews, a U.S. Supreme Court justice, and Harrison Gray Otis, the owner and publisher of the *Los Angeles Times*.

The 23rd OVI first served in (West) Virginia and then in the fall of 1862, at the Battles of South Mountain and Antietam during Lee's first invasion of the North. Ohioan General Jacob Dolson Cox ordered the 23rd OVI to attack the Confederate forces at Fox's Gap on South Mountain on September 14, 1862, as Bissland noted:

> *Cox ordered Col. Rutherford B. Hayes and his 23rd Ohio to lead the attack, hitting the Confederates at their strongest point. Yelling "Give them hell! Give the sons of bitches hell!" Hayes spurred his horse forward. Heavy*

fire forced his Ohioans to pause three times, but they reformed and charged again. Hayes was about to order a fourth charge when a bullet hit his left arm just above the elbow, breaking a bone and leaving a gaping hole. Feeling faint, Hayes sank to the ground. A wounded Confederate lay nearby and the two enemies had a friendly conversation as the battle raged all around them. Hayes asked the Confederate to send a message to Lucy Hayes if he died on the battlefield. During a pause in the battle, however, Hayes was rescued by his men.

At the fight at Burnside's Bridge at Antietam, future U.S. president William McKinley won recognition:

Conspicuous for his gallantry was William McKinley of the 23rd Ohio. By this time McKinley's diligence and attention to detail had won him the post of commissary sergeant. At Antietam, McKinley drove his wagon through enemy fire to bring coffee and food to the fighting men.

In July 1863, the 23rd OVI took part in the chase and capture of John Hunt Morgan's raiders in Southern Ohio. Morgan crossed the Ohio River just west of Cincinnati on July 13, according to Bissland:

Morgan kept his men in the saddle an average of twenty-one hours a day. Some fell asleep while riding, and some dropped out. Bushwhackers shot at them from hiding places and civilians burned bridges and felled trees to block roads. When they weren't fighting off Ohio soldiers and militia, the raiders roared into terrified towns to ransack stores, rip up railroad tracks, and capture horses to replace their own exhausted animals. Heading east across southern Ohio and having done all the damage he could, Morgan planned to escape across the Ohio River to reach friends waiting in (West) Virginia.

On July 26, Morgan and the remnants of his command surrendered near Lisbon after the Battle of Buffington Island before they could re-cross the Ohio River. This was the only engagement fought in Ohio during the Civil War. Morgan later escaped from imprisonment in the Ohio State Penitentiary in Columbus.

In the fall of 1864, the 23rd OVI participated in Phil Sheridan's Shenandoah Campaign, where Hayes, a brigade commander then, was again injured at the Battle of Cedar Creek, as described by Thomas Lewis:

23rd Ohio Volunteer Infantry (OVI) color guard. *Courtesy of Ohio History Connection.*

The fleeing infantry left Colonel Hayes behind, sitting on his horse dumbfounded and in mortal peril. He wheeled his mount to the rear and spurred to a gallop, apparently planning to get ahead of his men again, so he could try to rally them. He had gone only a few yards when a bullet tore into the horse, killing it instantly. In the sudden, heavy fall, Hayes was knocked momentarily unconscious, and when he came to had a searing pain in one ankle. He struggled to his feet and saw the enemy battle line rolling toward him. Finding to his relief that he could walk on the injured leg, Hayes started hobbling to the rear only to hear a shouted, profane demand that he halt and surrender. The Confederates caught up with him. Hayes forgot the pain, and ran. He dodged into a grove of trees, eluding the charging enemy soldiers for the moment, and kept running. A spent bullet came spinning down out of the roaring air and slammed him on the head; he staggered, stunned, but kept running. Eventually, he caught up with his staff, commandeered a horse, remounted, and started looking for a way to stop the rout.

Above: Cuyahoga County Infantry Regiment (23rd OVI) in Public Square, 1865. *Courtesy of Cleveland Memory Project, Michael Schwartz Library, Cleveland State University.*

Left: 23rd OVI Monument, Woodland Cemetery, Cleveland, Ohio. *Photo by Kay L. Martin.*

Opposite: 23rd OVI Monument marker, Woodland Cemetery, Cleveland Ohio. *Photo by Kay L. Martin.*

This was the seemingly lost battle turned into victory after Sheridan's famous ride to rejoin and lead his army in a victorious counterattack. After the battle, Hayes was promoted to brigadier general by Sheridan.

The regiment included 341 Clevelanders. It lost 159 (including 5 officers) in battle and 131 to disease (including an officer). The regiment was mustered out in 1865.

There are two monuments commemorating the 23rd OVI. The first was dedicated in July 1865 at Cleveland's Woodland Cemetery, one of the early Union Civil War monuments. A historical marker was placed near the monument in the cemetery in 2017. The second was dedicated in 1903 on the Antietam battlefield.

124TH OVI

The 124th OVI was organized in Cleveland; 567 of its total were Clevelanders. Its Company H was mostly recruited from Cleveland, and its Company C was mostly from Cuyahoga County and included many Irish. It served in the Army of the Cumberland throughout the war and was nicknamed the "Mice." Its first battle was Chickamauga, serving in the brigade commanded by General William Hazen. Its colonel, Clevelander Oliver Hazard Payne, was seriously wounded. Captain George W. Lewis, the regiment's historian, led Company B and told of a fellow soldier's death:

Corporal William Atkins, an ardent abolitionist and former schoolteacher who liked to preach the evils of slavery around the campfire, squeezed off a shot from behind a pine tree next to Lewis. A moment later a bullet tore open his left shoulder. Lewis was aghast. "William, you are badly wounded, go to the rear," he said with as much authority as he could muster. Atkins was not listening, the fever of battle had taken hold of him. Extending his bloody left arm toward Lewis, he replied: "See captain, I am not much hurt. I want to give them another." Lewis merely watched Atkins draw another cartridge from his box, run it down the barrel of this rifle, and then fall backward dead when a second bullet ripped through his chest.

James Garfield's action at the Battle of Chickamauga would be a major event in his ascent to the presidency. Garfield was born in 1831 in a log cabin near Cleveland. Born in poverty, he rose to become the twentieth president of the United States. After working on a canalboat, he received a formal education and became a teacher and then president of what became Hiram College, where he had previously studied and taught and met his wife, Lucretia. Just prior to the Civil War, Garfield became a lawyer and served in the Ohio State Senate.

Shortly after the war began, Garfield volunteered for service. He expected to be named commander of the 7th OVI but was not chosen. Instead, he was appointed commander of the 42nd OVI, which he helped to recruit, according to Bissland:

By November [1861] *the regiment had reached full strength and was undergoing rigorous training by its schoolmaster commander. Garfield taught himself military basics by whittling a set of wooden blocks, which he maneuvered on his desk to simulate marching. Then he used the blocks to teach his officers, who spent six to eight exhausting hours a day ordering their awkward recruits back and forth across the alternately dusty and muddy fields of Camp Chase* [in Columbus].

Garfield became a general with his first and only battlefield command being successful in driving Confederate forces from Eastern Kentucky in early 1862. He fought at Shiloh on April 7, 1862, during the second day's defeat of the Confederates. After recovering from an illness, Garfield became chief of staff for Ohioan General William Rosecrans, commander of the Army of the Cumberland. Garfield's most notable service was to return to the field and George Thomas's defense that saved the army on September 20, 1863,

General James A. Garfield in uniform. *Courtesy of Library of Congress.*

at the Battle of Chickamauga while Rosecrans retreated to Chattanooga after his army's defeat, as noted by Cozzens in *This Terrible Sound*:

> *Garfield's six-mile ride from Rossville to the Snodgrass house was the highlight of his military career; apart from his assassination, it was perhaps the most memorable moment of his life. During the presidential campaign of 1880, Garfield's supporters inflated it into an event second only to Paul Revere's ride in its importance and unsurpassed in its danger.*

After the Union army's defeat at Chickamauga, the 124th OVI next participated in the battles to break the ensuing Confederate siege of Chattanooga. It was one of the regiments that scaled Missionary Ridge and routed the Confederates. It then fought in Sherman's Atlanta Campaign in 1864. After the capture of this key target, it was sent under General John Schofield to join George Thomas's forces defending Nashville against the threat posed by John Bell Hood's invasion of Tennessee. The regiment saw no combat after Hood's devastating defeat in December 1864. It lost 85 men (including 7 officers) in combat and 124 enlisted men to disease.

103RD OVI

The 103rd OVI was organized in Cleveland in August 1862, with 460 of its members from Cleveland and Cuyahoga County. It participated in the 1863 Knoxville and East Tennessee Campaigns, where it fought its first two battles. After that, it went to Georgia, serving under Ohioan General Jacob Dolson Cox in Sherman's Atlanta Campaign.

About 22 percent of the regiment were casualties at the Battle of Resaca, Georgia, on May 14, 1864. Its color guard of nine were all killed or wounded that day. The color sergeant who died first was Martin Streibler, a French-born resident of Cleveland. Two others were killed. They are all commemorated in the Soldiers' and Sailors' Monument on Public Square. Its designer, Levi Schofield, served in the regiment. Sergeant Chauncy W. Mead, Company E, who was wounded at Resaca, wrote from Marietta, Georgia, on June 24, 1864, that his company had only twenty-two men left out of ninety-eight when they left twenty-two months earlier.

After Atlanta was captured, the 103rd OVI became the provost guard of the 23rd Corps. While it was present for the Battles of Franklin and Nashville, Tennessee, in late 1864, it remained behind the lines. Its only other brush with combat was briefly at Spring Hill on November 29, 1864, the day before the Battle of Franklin, when it defended a battery of the 1st OLA as General Schofield's Army of the Ohio escaped past Hood's Army of Tennessee.

The 103rd OVI ended the war in North Carolina, where the 23rd Corps eventually joined Sherman's army in its march through the Carolinas ending with the surrender of Joseph Johnston's army. The regiment returned to Cleveland in June 1865, according to Dale Thomas:

> A train had brought the 103rd Infantry back to Cleveland. One out of every four soldiers did not make it home. The regiment had already been mustered out of service at Raleigh, North Carolina. The area around Union Depot was comfortably full of men and women, young and old. Sisters were there to see brothers, children to see fathers, parents to see their boys, sweethearts and wives to see their own. The scene differed from the cheering in September 1862 when the regiment left the city. The anxious crowd now stood silently as the soldiers climbed down from the freight cars.... The regiment cleaned up in a nearby washroom and then marched behind Leland's Band up Water and Superior Streets. Now the cheering started as the soldiers came to Public Square.

The 103rd OVI lost 139 (including 2 officers) in combat and 106 enlisted men to disease.

In his collection of letters home, Dale Thomas provided a picture of the war's impact in Cuyahoga County. Bell Irvin Wiley noted:

> *The form and content of* [soldiers'] *letters varied greatly with the background and character of the writers. Some were models of literary excellence done in beautiful script, while others were so crudely written and so full of misspellings as almost to defy deciphering.…It is not meant to imply that the polished missives were consistently superior to the roughhewn products in every respect, for sometimes the crudely scribbled and ungrammatical letters of semi-literate Yanks were absorbingly interesting, highly informative documents rich in humor and replete with original and colorful phrase.*

One of the featured soldiers in the Thomas letter collection is farmer Nathan Hawkins of Olmsted, who enlisted in the 103rd OVI, Company G. He was captured in Eastern Tennessee in January 1864. After learning of his capture, his wife, Lucy, sent this letter to his commander:

> *To my Dear Husband*
>
> *Dear Nate, it is bedtime but I am thinking of you. It had not occurred to me that you would be taken prisoner. It seems as if you might starve. You suffered so much at Knoxville, and surely the Rebs must be harder up than our forces if that could be. I do not know if you will ever see this letter, but if you do, you will know that your wife thinks of you. I know if you can write and let me know where you are, you will, and do hope you will be paroled or exchanged soon.*

She only learned after the war that he had died in the notorious Confederate prison camp at Andersonville, Georgia.

After the war, the veterans' association of the 103rd OVI established a campground in Sheffield Lake west of Cleveland. It still exists there, along with a museum.

37TH OVI

Germans were a major nationality group that came to Cleveland (although they were more numerous in Cincinnati). In the 1840s, they formed one-third of the new residents. In 1848–49, refugees from the unsuccessful revolution of 1848 in Germany arrived. They were antislavery and supported the

Union. An estimated 200,000 German Americans served in the Union armies. Wiley observed:

> [On] *the whole the contribution of this nationality to the Union cause was tremendous. Many Germans, and especially the Forty-eighters, were men of good education and refined tastes whose influence improved the cultural tone of the units to which they belonged. Their technical aptitude and skill helped meet specialist needs in artillery, engineer and signal units. The prior training of many of them in European organizations was utilized for instruction of vast levies of green recruits.*

The 37th OVI was the first Ohio infantry regiment composed primarily of German Americans. Three of its companies were composed of Clevelanders. After serving initially in (West) Virginia in 1862, it went west. It participated in the Vicksburg Campaign under Grant. Serving in Ohioan Hugh Ewing's brigade, it fought in Grant's unsuccessful assaults on Vicksburg on May 19 and 22, 1863. Its commander was wounded. Some of its members volunteered to serve in the "Forlorn Hope" that paved the way and were awarded the Medal of Honor. There is a monument to the regiment on the Vicksburg battlefield marking the assaults.

It then participated in the battle of Missionary Ridge, lifting the Siege of Chattanooga. In the charge, John S. Kountz of Company G was charged with disobedience for throwing down his drum and joining the assault on the Confederate fortifications. He was severely wounded, and his leg was amputated. He was later awarded the Medal of Honor. In 1885, Kountz served as the national commander-in-chief of the Grand Army of the Republic.

The regiment then served in Sherman's Atlanta Campaign, March to the Sea and Carolinas Campaign. In total, 153 Clevelanders served in the regiment; 9 of its members won the Medal of Honor; 102 (including 9 officers) died from combat; and 95 (including an officer) died from disease.

41st OVI

The 41st OVI was organized from Northern Ohio, with Company D mostly from Cleveland, as described by Kimberley and Holloway. When it was organized, the regiment recruited a Cleveland band:

> *Jack Leland's band had a name in Cleveland long before the war. The leader joined and enlisted his men, and all entered with good heart upon the service. But the army band practice was not the same as that which the*

men were accustomed to, and when, some months after the regiment had gone to the field, the colonel called for a detail to blow the bugle, the leader explained that such service would "spoil the lip" of the man detailed. The colonel failed to appreciate the nicety of this objection, and a discouragement came upon the band.

As a result, the regiment lost its Cleveland band.

One of its recruits was businessman Emerson Opdycke. He would rise from private to command of the 125th OVI, which he recruited. At the Battle of Chickamauga, it would earn the name "Opdycke's Tigers." Opdycke's Tigers became heroes at the battle of Franklin, Tennessee, on November 30, 1864, when their counterattack stopped a desperate Confederate assault on the Army of the Ohio.

As Bissland describes, the first major battle for the 41st OVI was at Shiloh, Tennessee, on April 7, 1862, where nearly half of its total number of soldiers were killed or wounded, including Emerson Opdycke:

Acting Major Emerson Opdycke distinguished himself by seizing the regiment's colors after the color-bearer had fallen, and shouting, "Forty-First Ohio, follow your colors!" He was wounded twice. "To go over our…ground now, it seems miraculous how one of us escaped," Opdycke wrote his wife. "On Monday morning, I was within a few inches of thousands of whistling bullets, cannon balls, and bursting shells." He mentioned that his son's picture "was in my coat pocket during the battle, a little charm for me."

James McPherson noted a similar phenomenon: "But many of them [Civil War soldiers] did carry pocket Bibles or New Testaments, and numerous are the Civil War stories of a Bible in a breast pocket stopping a bullet."

McPherson also told from soldiers' letters of many getting religion during the war. For example, a young corporal in the 103rd Ohio wrote home in May 1864 that for the first time "I feel confident that I have found grace in the sight of god…why then should we be afraid to die." McPherson also said, "If there was one vice in Sherman's army that was more prevalent than all the others, it was swearing." This offended the more religious soldiers and officers. During the Carolinas Campaign, General Oliver Otis Howard, notable for his pious personality, called for an end to "the gross and criminal practice of profane swearing."

In 1862 came the Battle of Perryville, Kentucky. After that, the 41st OVI was assigned to the Army of the Cumberland and fought with it throughout most of the rest of the war. At the Battle of Stone's River, Tennessee, on December 31, 1862, the 41st held the line, losing one-fourth of its number as casualties. A monument on the battlefield marks its brigade's position. At Chickamauga in September 1863, it joined the final resistance to Confederate attacks on the remaining Union forces under General George Thomas on Horseshoe Ridge. There is a monument to it on the battlefield.

In Sherman's 1864 Atlanta Campaign, the regiment began with 331 men, and when it concluded, only 99 were present for duty, noted Kimberley and Holloway:

> One hundred and fifty had fallen in battle and more than 80 had succumbed to disease. No other campaign in the middle West equaled this one in duration, in marching service, and in frequent and close contact with the enemy. Many a day when there was no battle, it was a picket fight for breakfast, a skirmish for dinner, and another little fight to finish the day. For week after week, the din of musketry was ringing in the ears without cessation, save in the night; and the night still was often broken by marching or entrenching, or standing to arms. Those were a hundred days of uninterrupted strain, with none but the commonest indispensable supplies, and those not always regular and in full quantity. The marvel was that anything at all got over so long a line of supply.

Its last battle was again under General George Thomas in the defense of Nashville, Tennessee, in December 1864, which resulted in the virtual destruction of the Confederate Army of Tennessee. Its service ended in Texas. A total of 407 Clevelanders served in the regiment. It suffered 176 combat deaths, had 134 wounded and lost 141 to disease. Company D from Cleveland had 6 killed, 10 who died of wounds and 10 dead from disease. Two of the members of the 41st OVI won the Medal of Honor.

2ND OHIO VOLUNTEER CAVALRY (OVC)

The 2nd OVC was organized in Cleveland. Its initial quartermaster was John Johnson Elwell, a Cleveland doctor and lawyer. It served in Missouri (fighting the infamous Ohio-born rebel guerrilla William Quantrill), Kansas (chasing the Confederate general and Cherokee chief Stand Watie), Kentucky and Eastern Tennessee. Under German-born August Kautz, it pursued Morgan's Raiders in Ohio in 1863 until their capture. After the war, Kautz served on the board that investigated the assassins of President Lincoln. He also married the daughter of former Ohio governor David Tod.

The 2nd OVC served in the Eastern Theater with the Army of the Potomac in the 1864 Overland Campaign. Captain Henry Chester remembered:

> [On] *June 1st* [1864] *in one of the charges, we captured a rebel lieutenant who asked "To whom he had the honor of surrendering?" "2d Ohio" was the reply. Great Heavens! I fought that Regiment in the Indian Territory in Arkansas, in Kentucky, in Tennessee and now they have got me in Virginia.*

It fought under Phil Sheridan in his Shenandoah Valley Campaign in the fall of 1864, serving in General George Armstrong Custer's brigade. Under Sheridan's command, it pursued Lee's army's retreat from Richmond to its surrender at Appomattox. Altogether, it fought in eight battles and thirty skirmishes; 317 of its total members were Clevelanders. The regiment lost 83 (including 7 officers) in combat and 184 (including 5 officers) to disease.

On March 5, 1862, about one hundred men from the regiment, many of whom were from Cleveland, in winter quarters in Columbus destroyed the office of an anti-Lincoln Democratic newspaper (the *Crisis*). This reflected the pro-Lincoln support by a majority of Union soldiers during the war. No soldier was ever prosecuted or disciplined.

The wide-ranging campaigns of the 2nd OVC can be followed in the wartime diary of Luman Harris Tenney. He and some other Oberlin College friends enlisted in 1861. Tenney was appointed commissary sergeant of Company H. He regularly wrote about the food supplied to his company. He was also a regular forager during campaigns, finding fruits and vegetables in the countryside. Tenney had horses shot from under him. He ended the war as captain of Company C. Tragically, his brother Theodore was killed at the Battle of Five Forks, Virginia, just eight days before Lee's surrender. Luman heard his brother's last words and buried him on the battlefield. Tenney was praised by Custer, viewed President Lincoln's body in the White House after the assassination and participated in the Grand Review of the Armies in May 1865.

Tenney was an avid reader. He also played chess constantly. He corresponded often with a female friend named Fannie Andrews back in Oberlin, wondering whether she loved him. According to Wiley:

> *A substantial portion of letters written in camp* [by Union soldiers] *were addressed to sweethearts....Correspondence between soldiers and the girls they left behind were frequently formal and stilted, though now and then an established suitor would hazard the use of an endearing phrase.*

While on leave, Tenney paid several visits to Fannie. His diary entry for August 10, 1863, was as follows:

At 9:30 called on Fannie. [She] supposed I had gone. Interchanged sentiment, and agreeably. Happiest day of my life. Most fortunate boy. God grant it may cause no regret to either of us. Oh for grace to nobly do my part of life.

In Eastern Tennessee, Tenney made this entry in his diary on December 21, 1863: "[To] my unspeakable joy found a letter from Fannie, How long have I suffered from anxiety and suspense. I love the dear child more than ever, if such a thing be possible." Tenney married Fannie in April 1867, and they had four children. Tenney died in 1880.

Another history of the 2ⁿᵈ OVC is the *Recollections* of Henry W. Chester, written for his grandchildren long after the war. Chester was one of Tenney's Oberlin friends. He was born to a family of an abolitionist father on a farm east of Cleveland. His older brother Albert enlisted in the 1ˢᵗ OVC. Henry had risen from commissary sergeant (like Tenney) to captain by war's end. In 1864, near Petersburg, he was temporarily captured but escaped. On April 1, 1865, at the Battle of Five Forks, he witnessed the death of Theodore Tenney, Luman's brother. At Sailor's Creek on April 6, 1865, the last major battle in the Appomattox Campaign, Chester had a bullet graze his head, as described by a fellow officer:

Suddenly a man steps from behind a tree, takes deliberate aim and fires. Capt. Chester falls from his horse to the ground and the man throws down his musket and pleads for quarter....The coward is permitted to live and may repent his dastardly deed. On his knees. Captain Tenney, a comrade of Chester's at Oberlin College, gathers the fallen man in his arms, while others dress his wound, and are overjoyed to find that the ball has struck his forehead and glanced and stunned and not killed one of the bravest and worthiest men that ever-sought reputation at the cannon's mouth.

While serving in the West, Chester recounted learning the game of "LaCross" from pro-Union Indians. The 2ⁿᵈ OVI also learned the Indian war whoop, which it adopted as its own and made when it charged. It became known as the "2ⁿᵈ Ohio yell." In 1864, in the Shenandoah Valley Campaign, Chester remembered his admiration for General George Armstrong Custer, the daring commander of the cavalry division in which the 2ⁿᵈ OVI served.

At the Grand Review on May 23, 1865, Custer's division led the parade of the Army of the Potomac. His soldiers, including those of the 2nd OVC, wore "Red Ties" in honor of Custer.

1ST OHIO LIGHT ARTILLERY (OLA)

A total of 829 men from Cuyahoga County served in the 1st OLA's twelve batteries with Batteries A and B from the Cleveland Light Artillery. It was commanded by James Barnett, Cleveland businessman and member of the Cleveland Grays. Barnett's family moved to Cleveland in 1825. He became a successful businessman with ties to banking, railroads and mining. He joined the Cleveland Grays in 1839 and in 1856 helped to organize the Republican Party in Cleveland. From command of the Cleveland Light Artillery, during the Civil War he commanded the 1st Ohio Light Artillery. Barnett was the highest-ranked officer from Cleveland to serve in the Union army during the Civil War. After the war, Barnett was appointed police commissioner in 1866 and served on the Cleveland City Council in 1873–74. Barnett also served on the board of managers for the Soldiers' and Sailors' Orphan Home in Xenia, Ohio, and the National Homes for Disabled Soldiers. There is a monument to him at the Erie Street Cemetery and a bust of him in the Soldiers' and Sailors' Monument.

At the Battle of Chancellorsville in 1863, German-born Hubert Dilger, captain of its Battery I, won the Medal of Honor. At the Battle of Gettysburg, the 1st OLA fought with the 11th Corps. There are monuments in Gettysburg to three of its batteries: I, K and L. During the Atlanta Campaign, Captain Hubert Dilger's Battery I was credited with firing the long-distance round on June 14, 1864, that killed Confederate lieutenant general and corps commander of the Army of Tennessee Leonidas Polk (the "Bishop General"). During the war, this unit lost a total of 84 in combat and 385 from disease. One of the 10 wounded from Battery K, commanded by German baker Lewis Heckman at the Battle of Gettysburg, was Private William H. Cobbledick from Cleveland.

Cobbledick, an Englishman by birth, sustained a hand wound but remained on duty. During Gettysburg's fiftieth battle anniversary reunion in 1913, he claimed, at age ninety, to be the oldest Ohio veteran in attendance, as noted by Richard Baumgartner.

125TH OVI (5TH USCT)

Despite opposition, President Lincoln was persuaded to have free African Americans, including emancipated former slaves, join the Union army.

They would serve in all-Black regiments of the United States Colored Troops (USCT). In Ohio, Governor David Tod supported the recruitment of Black soldiers.

Arming Blacks to serve in the Union army, led by White officers, was very controversial. Many Union army officers and soldiers initially objected. A leading advocate was Frederick Douglass, who lobbied President Lincoln for equal pay for the soldiers of the USCT, according to Edward Achorn:

> *Douglass continued urging black men to fight, despite their lower pay, few to no opportunities for advancement in the ranks, and a far grimmer disadvantage: the serious risk of being executed or sold back into slavery if captured by the Confederates. He recognized that if black men fought to save the nation, they would be making an almost unanswerable argument for full citizenship.*
>
> *For much of Ohio's history, African Americans had been regarded as almost subhuman, to be feared, despised, and marginalized, and it has been observed that the state's first black regiment was "gotten up on the cheap to save white Ohioans from the draft." But it was another step forward in black Americans' long journey toward equality, a step that black leader John Mercer Langston predicted would "challenge the respect and admiration of the world."…At first, Governor Tod opposed Langston's raising a black regiment for Ohio, but by mid-June 1863 Tod had an epiphany: black enlistees could help meet the state's draft quota just as well as whites.*
>
> *Previously, Clevelander John Malvin, a leader in the Black community, had organized a company that joined the first two Black regiments in Massachusetts. The first Black Ohio regiment was the 127th OVI, which became the 5th USCT.*

It was commanded by Giles Shurtleff. After his release from capture in 1861 and imprisonment in several Confederate prisons, Shurtleff returned to Oberlin College and wrote:

> *I rejoice to learn how thoroughly the cruel hatred of the black race is being dispelled. I regard the movement in this direction by far the most encouraging aspect of the war. God bless the negroes and make them wise and prudent in this time of their great deliverance. If I was going into the field, I should feel tempted to ask for command of colored troops.*

Above: 127th OVI, 5th United States Colored Troops. *Courtesy of Ohio History Connection.*

Right: Giles Waldo Shurtleff, 1861. *Courtesy of Oberlin College Civil War Archives.*

On July 29, 1863, Governor Tod appointed Shurtleff second in command of the 127th OVI.

In September 1864, Shurtleff took over command of what was now the 5th USCT regiment. He led it into battle on September 29, 1864, as the Union Army of the James under General Ben Butler before Richmond began its assault on New Market Heights. As the regiment charged the Confederate works, Shurtleff was shot in his right hand and his thigh. Besides Shurtleff, the 5th USCT suffered 235 casualties, including 28 killed. In recognition of Shurtleff's gallantry, Butler promoted him to colonel. Four of its Black soldiers were awarded the Medal of Honor for their bravery in this battle at Chaffin's Farm when they led their companies after their White officers were killed or wounded.

The 5th USCT was next sent to North Carolina as part of Butler's expedition to capture Fort Fisher. However, it was assigned to capture the port of Wilmington, guarded by the fort. Butler failed, but a subsequent assault by General Alfred Terry did result in the capture of the fort. And on February 22, 1865, Union troops captured Wilmington. That ended the 5th USCT's wartime combat service.

It joined General Sherman's army at Goldsboro after it marched into North Carolina and effectively ended the war by forcing the surrender of General Joseph Johnston's force in April 1865, according to Joseph Glatthaar:

By the time Sherman's army reached Goldsboro, North Carolina, it was in all its glory. Hatless heads, threadbare shirts, torn shoes or barefoot, faces blackened by the Carolinas pine smoke, they looked, as a member of Schofield's army noted, "very hard."

The 5th USCT regiment lost a total of 249 during its service; 4 officers and 77 enlisted men were killed or mortally wounded, and 2 officers and 166 men died of disease.

Versalle Washington noted that Colonel Shurtleff left for Oberlin, giving this farewell address:

The relation which has so long existed between you and myself is severed. For nearly two years your interests have been my interests. Together we have had our part in hard marches, trying sieges, and bloody battles. Together we have wept over fallen comrades— together rejoiced in successes achieved and victories won. Your record is one of which you may well be proud. God will reward you for your sacrifices and a grateful country appreciates your

Giles Waldo Shurtleff statue, Oberlin, Ohio. *Photo by Kay L. Martin.*

service. Thanking you for your uniform kindness and prompt obedience, I bid you an affectionate farewell.

There is a statue of Shurtleff in Oberlin. Its inscription reads:

Believing in the ability of the negro to aid in his fight for his freedom, he organized the first regiment of colored troops in Ohio. Inspired by his leadership they offered their lives for the freedom of their race.

While not all Union officers and soldiers appreciated the sacrifices of the USCT and did not support the army's support for fugitive slaves, there were notable exceptions, according to Bell Irvin Wiley:

Interest in promoting the educational and spiritual progress of the colored folk was especially strong among soldiers of antislavery background. An Ohio company made up of Oberlin College boys sent one of the first fugitives who came under their control to Oberlin for education.

After the surrender of Richmond in April, the first Union troops to enter the Confederate capital were those of the USCT, under the command of Ohioan General Godfrey Weitzel.

8TH OVI

The 8th OVI from Northern Ohio was organized in the spring of 1861. It became known as the "Fighting Fools." Company B was from Cleveland and was known as the Hibernian Guards. In 1862, the 8th OVI first fought in (West) Virginia and then against Stonewall Jackson in the Shenandoah Valley. Then it joined the Army of the Potomac. At Antietam on September 17, 1862, facing Robert E. Lee's invading Confederates, the 8th OVI suffered heavy losses when it attacked the "Bloody Lane," where there is today a statue commemorating its valor. In Sergeant Thomas Galwey's Company B, only four men, including young Galwey, out of thirty-two remained unhurt, according to Bissland:

Galwey and the 8th Ohioans vaulted fences and filed through an apple orchard until Confederate riflemen popped up from the Sunken Road and fired at them. Men around Galwey began to drop. With no reinforcements to help them, Galwey told his diary, the Ohioans "go forward on the run, heads downward as if under a pelting rain." Heavy fire forced them to pause about fifty yards from the Sunken Road. "Our men are falling by the hundreds," Galwey wrote.…The 8ᵗʰ Ohio was ordered to charge again, but intense Confederate fire drove it back. Attempting its fourth or fifth attack, the Union brigade fixed bayonets and charged the Sunken Road again. "We raise a savage yell and advance on the run," Galwey wrote, and this time they reached the road, only to find it abandoned by the Confederates.

For its bravery, its brigade was named the "Gibraltar Brigade" by the corps commander, Edwin Sumner.

Next that year was the Battle of Fredericksburg, Virginia, in December. The Army of the Potomac suffered tremendous casualties, but the 8ᵗʰ OVI was not heavily engaged. One of the Confederates killed was General Maxcy Gregg, whose South Carolinians had ambushed the 1ˢᵗ Ohio in Vienna, Virginia, in 1861.

In 1863, after the Battle of Chancellorsville, the 8ᵗʰ OVI found itself much reduced in number at the Battle of Gettysburg. On the third day, it was on the flank of the Union defense against the Pickett-Pettigrew charge. It attacked a Confederate brigade and captured several hundred prisoners while suffering almost 50 percent casualties, including its commander Franklin Sawyer, as Bissland noted:

Among the 8ᵗʰ Ohio's wounded was Capt. Azor H. Nickerson [also wounded at the Battle of Antietam], *shot through one arm and his lungs. Carried behind the lines in a blanket, he had been left lying on Cemetery Ridge. Struggling to his feet, blood gushed from his mouth and he fainted. He awoke in a roughly bouncing ambulance that took him to a makeshift hospital in a barn. "I am not afraid to hear the worst; is there any hope for me, doctor?" Nickerson asked a surgeon. "No," the surgeon said, patting him gently on the forehead and looking away. "No, none whatsoever." To Nickerson's amazement, he would not only survive after a long convalescence, but also return to Gettysburg months later.*

Richard Baumgartner noted that Nickerson returned to hear President Lincoln deliver his Gettysburg Address on November 19, 1863, dedicating the National Cemetery:

Thirty years afterward Nickerson declared…I thought then, and still think, it was the shortest, grandest speech, sermon, or what you please to call it, to which I ever listened.…My own emotions may perhaps be imagined

*when it is remembered he was facing the spot where only a short time before
we had our death grapple with Pickett's men, and where he stood almost
immediately over the place where I had lain [July 3] and seen my comrades
torn in fragments by the enemy's cannon-balls.*

Seventeen soldiers from the 8th OVI and six from the 1st OLA (Light
Artillery) were buried in the Ohio section of the cemetery.

Two soldiers of the 8th OVI won the Medal of Honor in this battle. A
monument, dedicated on September 14, 1887, with thirty-seven of its
veterans present, stands near where it fought at Gettysburg, commemorating
its remarkable bravery:

*According to Lieutenant Galwey, "As we ascended the hill down which we
had come yesterday in gallant array, the artillery, who had seen us throughout
the fight, cheered us and spoke flattering words to us as we passed them."
Captain John Madeira, a 73rd Ohio officer serving on Colonel Orlando
Smith's brigade staff, had watched the "distinguished work" of Sawyer's
troops from the side of Cemetery Hill. Unaware of their identity, Madeira
rode over to investigate. "I never was so proud of being an Ohio man in my
life when I found that the men whose gallantry I had never seen eclipsed on
a battlefield was the Eighth Ohio. I felt like yelling out, 'I'm from Ohio,
too! Bully for Ohio!'"*

In the spring of 1864, the 8th OVI took part in Grant's Overland Campaign
against Lee. At the Battle of Spotsylvania Court House, it took part in an
innovative Union assault at the Bloody Angle, and another one of its soldiers
won the Medal of Honor. Lieutenant Thomas Galwey, then the commander
of Company B, wrote:

*Nothing can describe the confusion, the savage blood curdling yells, the
murderous faces, the awful curses, super human hardihood, and the grisly
horror of the melee! Of all the battles I took part in, Bloody Angle at
Spotsylvania exceeded all of the rest in stubbornness, ferocity, and in
courage. I cannot understand how any of us survived it.*

Reaching Petersburg, the regiment was withdrawn and returned to
Cleveland on July 3, 1864, to be mustered out. Out of a total of 990 who
began their service with the unit, 97 men were present. During the war, the
8th OVI lost 132 (including 8 officers) in battle and 73 (including an officer)

Ohio at Gettysburg Monument to the 8th OVI. *Courtesy of Ohio History Connection.*

to disease. Company B suffered 45 casualties out of its wartime total of 101 members.

The experience of the soldiers of the 8th OVI can be better understood through the wartime diary of Thomas Francis Galwey (excerpts to follow). Galwey's previous comments about his experience with the Hibernian Guards of the 8th OVI at the Battles of Antietam, Gettysburg and Spotsylvania Court House reflect his heroic service in the Civil War.

Following the announcement of the Confederate bombardment of Fort Sumter, the next day Galwey and a friend went to enlist. They first visited the armory of the Cleveland Grays. However, Galwey said, "They did not seem to be the sort of stuff that soldiers are made of, so I went away." Instead, Galwey and two friends enlisted with the Hibernian Guards. Galwey was only fifteen years old.

His Company B of the 8th OVI was mustered in for three months service at Camp Taylor in Cleveland. In May 1861, the regiment then went by train to Camp Chase outside Columbus for training. Galwey signed up for a three-year enlistment and, after a furlough in Cleveland, returned to find that he had been made second sergeant of his company.

~~~

In July, the 8th OVI was sent to (West) Virginia, serving under General George McClellan's forces from Ohio. Its first assignment was pursuit of a retreating Confederate force:

> *On Tuesday the 16th [July 1861] we are still marching. I would give anything for relief from carrying my knapsack. The other men are full of terrible oaths and threats, nearly a fourth of them straggling for miles back along the road. Those of us who keep up with the column, toiling along footsore and aching in every bone, are tempted every moment to join the stragglers. This business of marching is new to us; we haven't been trained for nor hardened to it.*

Its next unpleasant experience in the field was camp fever and dysentery that swept through the regiment. Galwey found:

> *Our company, the only one composed of men from the city, was scarcely affected at all, showing that countrymen are not more hardy than city boys.*

According to Wiley:

In its initial attacks illness fell with unusual vehemence on rural units. Prior exposure to contagious disease and a more favorable attitude toward vaccination gave greater immunity to city-reared soldiers.

On October 26, 1861, the Union troops achieved their objective of capturing the town of Romney. The company of Hibernian Guards was assigned as skirmishers. The commander of the 8th OVI resigned. Major Franklin Sawyer temporarily took command until the arrival of West Pointer Samuel Carroll, who arrived on December 16 to take command. Galwey reported that many of his fellow soldiers got drunk. As a sergeant of the Guard, Galwey had to deal with the death of a soldier found after a drunken brawl. After a retreat, Galwey was sent to Columbus in February 1862 on recruiting duty.

~~~

When Galwey rejoined the 8th OVI, it had been reassigned to the Army of the Potomac's Second Corps. During his absence, it got its first battle experience in the Shenandoah Valley at the first Battle of Kernstown outside Winchester. The defeated Confederates had been led by General Thomas "Stonewall" Jackson.

The Union army division in which the 8th OVI served was led by Irish-born General James Shields. He was a lawyer and served in the Illinois legislature. In 1842, he almost fought a duel with Abraham Lincoln. Shields was a twice-wounded veteran of the Mexican-American War. After that, he moved to Minnesota, founded the town of Shieldsville and was elected senator (after previously serving as a senator and also a member of the Supreme Court in Illinois). Shields was also wounded at the Battle of Kernstown. After a promotion was later withdrawn, Shields resigned from the army. In 1866, he moved to Missouri and in 1879 temporarily served in the U.S. Senate again. His statue from Illinois stands in the National Statuary Hall at the U.S. Capitol; there is also a statue on the grounds of the Minnesota state capitol in St. Paul.

The regiment was next sent to join Ohioan Irvin McDowell's force opposite Fredericksburg, Virginia. Galwey described his fellow soldiers thusly:

By now we look like a pack of thieving vagabonds—no crowns in our hats, no soles to our shoes, no seats to our pantaloons. We make a good foil to the sleek, well-fed soldiers of McDowell's corps who are occupying Fredericksburg. After much trouble we draw some shoes and other necessities, but before we have a chance to show ourselves to McDowell's troops in our new attire we are hurried back to the Shenandoah Valley.

Now commanded by Franklin Sawyer after Samuel Carroll was promoted to lead a brigade, the 8th OVI surprised a Confederate force at Front Royal on June 1, 1862, capturing about three hundred prisoners. Galwey reported:

During our stay here I was introduced to the famous Belle Boyd, a Confederate female spy who had been taken prisoner when we captured the town. She is rather handsome and has some accomplishments although their luster is somewhat heightened by her rather romantic career.

Boyd began her spying career in 1861, when her slave was caught carrying a message from her to the Confederates. In 1862, by eavesdropping in May on Shields's plans and relaying them to General Stonewall Jackson, she did help the Confederate army. Jackson made her an honorary aide-de-camp as a reward. Pursued by Pinkerton detectives, she was arrested on July 29, 1862, and jailed in the Old Capital Prison in Washington City. She was sent to Fort Monroe, Virginia, and released on August 29 in an exchange. Boyd was captured in March 1864 trying to reach England when she was caught by the Union sea blockade. In Canada, she met a Union naval officer, and they married in England. After the war, Boyd wrote a two-volume memoir, *Belle Boyd in Camp and Prison.*

On June 9, 1862, the 8th OVI fought Jackson's army again at the Battle of Port Republic. Having defeated the Union army led by General John C. Frémont the previous day at Cross Keys, Jackson also defeated forces under Shields commanded by General Erastus Tyler, while Frémont was unable to come to their aid. These two Confederate victories ended Jackson's remarkable Shenandoah Valley Campaign. This allowed Confederate control of the Valley, while Jackson was able to join Robert E. Lee's army defending the Confederate capitol of Richmond, which was threatened by George McClellan's Army of the Potomac.

~~~

The 8th OVI was shipped to Harrison's Landing on the James River to join the Army of the Potomac. It arrived on July 1 as McClellan's army repelled the

Confederate attack at Malvern Hill, ending the Seven Days Battles in which Robert E. Lee had rallied the Confederate army and defeated McClellan's advance on Richmond. The 8th OVI engaged in some skirmishing with the Confederates over the next few days. On July 8, President Lincoln visited the army, but Galwey's regiment did not see him. Galwey reported on the conditions at their camp:

> *Owing to the bad water, everyone fell sick with diarrhea. Quinine is given us in great quantity. Onions, too, are sent from Washington, for we have much scurvy from bad food. The heat is terrible. We take off all our clothing to escape it, and then the flies swarm all over us. I have never seen such flies, and in such enormous numbers. Without exaggeration, the tents are as black as ink owing to them. At night we sleep on the open parade ground and by companies curse the heat.*

The 8th OVI and the Army of the Potomac left the Peninsula to return to Northern Virginia, with McClellan ordered to support General John Pope's army, which was faced with Lee's Army of Northern Virginia. Instead, when they arrived across from the capital, they met men from Pope's retreating army defeated at the Second Battle of Manassas. And then came news that Lee's army had crossed the Potomac into Maryland in an invasion of the North. Lee's aims were twofold: to recruit Marylanders to his army and to inflict a defeat on Union forces that would persuade European powers such as England and France to recognize the Confederacy.

As the Union army prepared to pursue Lee, Galwey recounted the condition of his unit:

> *They are issuing us shoes and fresh ammunition. We are very dirty and very lousy. The shirts we have on our backs now, we have worn for about a month. As our knapsacks are stored somewhere in Washington or Alexandria, there is little hope of changing our shirts until some very desperate or important movements have been made. We all scratch alike, generals and privates. The lice have grown to be perfect torture to us. While I was on picket one night, one of my men, a hard case but a jolly fellow, Jack Shepard, amused himself by stringing vermin on needle and thread for a necklace, gathering his jewels from the inside of the ankles of the mens' pantaloons. I can't imagine that anyone can become accustomed to lice.*

John Casement, commander of the 103rd OVI, also experienced this problem while on the 1864 Atlanta Campaign, as described by William Stark:

> *The heat, unfortunately, brought forth a host of vermin—woodticks, lice ("greybacks"), and insects—scorpions, maggots, common flies, ants, and sand flies. Colonel Casement enjoyed his leisure time scratching bites, becoming so efficient at it that it became unnecessary to unbutton any clothing to bring relief.*

Galwey expressed bitterness at the opposition of Henry Halleck, the army's chief of staff, and Ohioan Edwin Stanton, the secretary of war, to the president's reappointment of George McClellan as the commander of the Army of the Potomac on September 2, 1862, after his failed Peninsula Campaign. Lincoln did this despite his previous statement that McClellan had the "slows" in confronting Lee and also McClellan's contempt for his war policies. Reflecting the views of most of his fellow soldiers, Galwey felt, "There is an air of uncertainty everywhere. But we have the greatest confidence in our gallant McClellan. If they leave him unhampered, he will bring things all right."

The Army of the Potomac marched north to meet Lee's invading army, with Galwey's unit passing through Frederick, Maryland, on September 13 to the cheers of the residents. That same day, a Union soldier found Lee's battle orders wrapped in three cigars in a field outside Frederick. They showed that Lee had divided his army into five segments. The discovery of this "Lost Order" gave McClellan the opportunity to defeat Lee's army in detail. McClellan informed President Lincoln that he was confident of defeating Lee. On Sunday, September 14, Galwey wrote, "[W]e resume the march. General McClellan, 'Little Mac' as we call him, passes us. He takes off his cap to us and we give him a hearty cheer. Few armies have felt an enthusiasm for their commanders such as we feel for ours."

The 8th OVI arrived at South Mountain west of Frederick too late to participate in the battle in which Union corps commander General Jessie Reno was killed and Rutherford B. Hayes, commander of the 23rd OVI, was wounded. It arrived at Antietam Creek and awoke on the morning of September 16 to a Confederate artillery shell that killed its color bearer.

Up early on September 17, the 8th OVI marched to join the already engaged Union corps of General Joseph Hooker (who was later wounded). It then, joined by the Irish Brigade, faced Confederates in a sunken lane. As previously recounted by Galwey, the fighting was fierce, as the Union soldiers repeatedly charged the entrenched Confederates. Galwey described the deaths of several of his comrades. After finally taking the Confederate position, the 8th OVI was relieved. Galwey was then hit by the explosion of a Confederate shell and permanently lost the hearing in his right ear.

After the bloodiest single day in American military history, Lee's army retreated back into Virginia. The 8th OVI helped to bury the dead. It then headed through the town of Sharpsburg, crossed the Potomac River and rested in Harper's Ferry. Before the Battle of Antietam, it had been captured by Stonewall Jackson, resulting in the largest surrender of Union troops during the war. On November 3, Galwey received his commission as a second lieutenant.

Since the Battle of Antietam, President Lincoln had been telling McClellan to engage Lee and destroy his outnumbered army. Lincoln visited McClellan at Sharpsburg on October 1–4 to personally deliver that message. But McClellan still did not cross the Potomac until October 26. Lincoln waited until after the November elections to relieve McClellan of command of the Army of the Potomac. The Democrat McClellan believed in fighting only a limited war and was not in favor of the emancipation of slaves. Based on McClellan's repulse of Lee's invasion, Lincoln had issued a Preliminary Emancipation Proclamation on September 22. It freed slaves only in those areas still held by the Confederates. It took full effect on January 1, 1863. According to Jonathan White, not all in the Union armies supported the proclamation, especially some who were Democrats. Interestingly, in his diary, Galwey said nothing about Lincoln's Emancipation Proclamation.

General Ambrose Burnside replaced McClellan. The soldiers' reactions, including that of Galwey, were mostly critical of Lincoln's action. Galwey described the last review of the army for McClellan before he departed:

> [W]e have reached the open plain, about a mile from our camp, selected for the review. There, in line of battalions en masse, we await the appearance of our adored commander. When he does appear, a half-shout and half-sob is heard throughout the lines. The very roughest and apparently most unfeeling men are red about the eyes. Strange exclamations of all sorts are heard. There are oaths, only partially repressed, ejaculations of affection, and wild yells of defiance at the loyal stay-at-homes and the Washington politicians. McClellan passes us, salutes our colors, cap in hand, smiling as usual. In spite of civilian machinations, he has reason to be proud of the devotion of men who have known him and have seen him in the time that tried men's souls.

~~~

Urged on by Lincoln, Burnside moved the Army of the Potomac to Falmouth on the Rappahannock River opposite the town of Fredericksburg. Burnside's plan was to advance toward Richmond before Lee was able to block the army. However, due to a delay in the arrival of pontoon boats, the Union army was unable to cross the river before Lee's army arrived and entrenched itself on the far bank. On December 12, the 8th OVI crossed the river under fire and found shelter in the abandoned town where Union soldiers were plundering, including some from Galwey's company. On December 13, Galwey's company was ordered to act as skirmishers west of the town. The men watched as wave after wave of Union troops valiantly but unsuccessfully tried to reach the stone wall on Marye's Heights above the town. This included the Irish Brigade,

> [w]hich comes out of the city in glorious style, their green sunbursts waving, as they waved on many a bloody battlefield before, in the thickest of the fight where the grim and thankless butchery of war is done. Every man has a sprig of green in his cap, and a half-laughing, half-murderous look in his eye. They pass just to our left, poor fellows, poor glorious fellows, shaking goodbye to us with their hats! They reach a point within stone's throw of the stone wall. No farther. They try to go beyond but are slaughtered. Nothing could advance farther and live. They lie down doggedly, determined to hold the ground they have already taken. There, away out in the fields to the front and left of us, we see them for an hour or so, lying in line close to that terrible stone wall.

About half of the Irish Brigade's 1,200 men were killed, wounded or went missing in its assault. In its most famous regiment, the 69th New York, 16 of 18 officers and 112 of 240 enlisted men were casualties. The Army of the Potomac suffered 13,000 casualties in this disastrous battle. When the losses of the Irish Brigade became known to the Irish community in New York City, anger grew at the feeling that the sacrifices of the Irish soldiers went unappreciated. This resentment was magnified when it was revealed that the War Department had denied its commander General Thomas Francis Meagher's request for a special leave to rest and recruit. Galwey's company recrossed the river days later in a rainstorm to discover that its quarters had been pillaged by camp followers (called "dog-robbers" and "pot whollopers").

~~~

After the Battle of Fredericksburg, Galwey described life in winter camp in Falmouth. There was picket duty in the snow. He described its winter quarters as comfortable:

The construction of these is very simple, yet they include every necessary convenience, often varied according to the artistic taste or the mechanical skill of the occupants. In general, each hut is made to accommodate a noncommissioned officer and from eight to twelve men. The walls, which are made of logs, are twelve to twenty feet long, from eight to ten feet wide, and about five feet high. At the middle of each end a forked stick supports a cross piece. Over this is stretched the shelter tents (of all the men) buttoned together. Usually, two thicknesses of tents are spread. This roof keeps out the rain and snow. The chimneys are sometimes made of sticks piled crosswise upon one another; sometimes and in fact more often, they are of pork barrels from the Commissary.

Galwey described the hearty dinners made available in camp:

The food issued to the soldiers is very good and in ample quantity. It consists of salt pork or fresh beef; soft bread baked in field ovens, and hard tack on the march and in campaign; coffee and sugar; for vegetables, desiccated potatoes; mixed desiccated vegetables for soup; and beans, rice, and onions. Besides these, we can buy from the sutler all sorts of delicacies such as oysters, canned fruit, cheese, raisins, tobacco, and last though not least, whisky. But whisky is generally sold on the sly.

Galwey described the celebration of St. Patrick's Day hosted by the Irish Brigade. Irish whiskey was featured. Galwey said that he "was satisfied with one large cup draught."

On January 20, 1863, Burnside opened a second offensive against Lee. It immediately bogged down in heavy rains, resulting in it being called the "Mud March." With its abject failure, several of Burnside's commanders conspired to have him relieved. Burnside responded by going to Lincoln and demanding their being dismissed or he would resign. After consulting Halleck and Stanton, Lincoln accepted Burnside's resignation, dismissed some of his critics and appointed Joseph Hooker to command the Army of the Potomac.

Hooker restored morale, and he planned an offensive against Lee for the spring of 1863. President Lincoln came to the army's camp on April 8 for a grand review. Galwey compared the appearance of the president with that of Joe Hooker:

> *President Lincoln wore a civilian suit of plain black* a la mode *"American gentleman," I suppose. The poor man looked very wan and pale, and cut an outrageously awkward figure on horseback, with his stovepipe hat and his elbows stuck out keeping time to the motion of his horse, while his chin seemed almost buried between the knees of his long bony legs. To make it worse, he rode alongside of General Hooker, our new commander, who is remarkably handsome and rides his horse like a centaur.*

Beginning on April 23, 1863, Galwey enjoyed a fifteen-day leave:

> *My return* [to Cleveland], *of course, caused great joy at home, although it had like to end fatally. My poor mother, after taking one long look at me and after kissing me, swooned away, and it was only to great care that we brought her to. I made the most of my time while on furlough. I visited many old friends, who seemed delighted to see me. They forced me again and again to explain certain movements in the army of which they had read but had been unable to understand thoroughly. Many of my friends, too, lifelong Democrats, had from the first been opposed to war and, in spite of old friendship, it was hard to hear tranquilly the many sarcastic remarks which they made in reference to the war.*

Just before Galwey left Cleveland to return to the army, he heard news of the Battle of Chancellorsville. General Joe Hooker planned to outflank Lee's vastly outnumbered army by crossing the Rappahannock and Rapidan Rivers, moving through a tangled forest called "the Wilderness" at the crossroads at Chancellorsville, and force Lee to fight in the open. On April 27, 1863, Hooker's army began this movement, while leaving a single corps at Fredericksburg in Lee's rear. Hooker boasted about destroying Lee's army. Initially, Hooker's plan worked, until he delayed moving out of the Wilderness, while Lee sent his army into it to block Hooker's advance. Lee and Stonewall Jackson then decided on a bold move. Lee divided his force, sending Jackson with about two-thirds of his troops on May 2 to attack Hooker's exposed right flank. While the largely German American 11th Corps warned General O.O. Howard about this looming threat, he ignored its warning. Jackson's force then routed Howard's corps. This victory was marred that night when Jackson was wounded by friendly fire. He would die on May 10. On May 3, as the Confederates renewed their attack, Hooker was stunned by a cannonball shot that hit his headquarters. Against the advice of several of his commanders, he refused to counterattack. On May 5–6, Hooker's army retreated, having suffered more than seventeen thousand casualties.

Upon his return to the army on May 14, Thomas Galwey was relieved to find that none of the soldiers in the 8th OVI had been among those casualties. On May 17, he described going on picket duty across the river from several Confederate regiments:

> *Our intercourse with the enemy's pickets, as soon as both sides understood that the lines were established for a time, was usually very friendly....I have seen men who had been sharpshooting one another desperately a few minutes before, come to the same fence for rails to cook their coffee, which they would cook in peace. Then they would contentedly munch their hard, mouldy crackers, cracking at the same time good-natured jokes at one another over the result of some late battle.*

~~~

Despite the loss of Jackson, Lee soon proposed a second invasion of the North intended to relieve Virginia from the ravages of war and to destroy the Army of the Potomac and win the war. With President Davis's approval, Lee assembled a reinforced army, which began its march north on June 10, 1863. By June 17, its vanguard was crossing the Potomac River again. By June 27, Confederate forces had entered Pennsylvania, with one corps headed toward the state capital at Harrisburg. Meanwhile, Hooker's army in Northern Virginia did not react quickly to Lee's masked advance. It wasn't until June 25 that it finally began to cross the Potomac in pursuit of Lee.

Galwey's regiment began moving north on June 14. While on the march, Galwey described soldiers gambling in a game called "Chuck-Luck," betting on the numbers of dice thrown on a blanket. On June 23, he noted, "Today I saw a twenty-acre field black with Chuck-Luck parties squatting on the grass." The 8th OVI crossed the Potomac on June 26. The next day, President Lincoln relieved Hooker of command of the Army of the Potomac. Lincoln replaced him with Pennsylvanian George Meade. Given the dissatisfaction in the army after the Chancellorsville defeat, Galwey thought that "maybe the change is good."

Galwey confessed to straggling on June 29 as the army marched rapidly north:

> *My feet are very sore. Generally, I am one of the best marchers in our company which, by the way, is considered one of the best marching companies in the brigade. Seldom is a Hibernian seen amongst the stragglers....Finally, I could not put one foot before another. I was utterly done out, so sticking my pass* [from a surgeon] *in my hat band, and telling my sergeant of my intentions, I stepped out from the ranks and lay down on a spot of grass in the angle of a fence. In a minute or two I dropped asleep.*

Early the next morning, Galwey caught up with his company. Galwey's exhaustion was understandable. In the heat and humidity of the summer, General Winfield Scott Hancock's Second Corps covered thirty-two miles on June 29–30.

The 8th OVI reached the Gettysburg battlefield the evening of July 1. They were met by soldiers from the 11th Corps, fleeing from its defeat that day. Lee's scattered army had converged despite his not wanting to bring on a battle yet, especially in the absence of good intelligence because Jeb Stuart's cavalry had not stayed with Lee's army as it headed north. After being held off temporarily by John Buford's Federal cavalry until General John Reynolds's 1st Corps arrived, the Confederates eventually sent Union soldiers fleeing through the streets of Gettysburg to seek refuge on Cemetery Hill, overlooking the town. Reynolds was killed. Second Corps commander General Hancock assumed command of that wing as the rest of the Army of the Potomac began to arrive.

The Gibraltar Brigade, including the 8th OVI, formed the next morning on Cemetery Ridge near the cemetery. July 2 saw the late afternoon attack by James Longstreet's Confederate corps, which crushed the exposed Union 3rd Corps, which had been unwisely placed beyond the Union lines by its commander, General Dan Sickles (who lost a leg). Heavy fighting took place in the Peach Orchard and the Wheatfield. That afternoon, the Hibernian Guards were ordered to drive Confederate skirmishers back from the Emmitsburg pike, from which they were harassing Union artillery batteries. This was accomplished. At the other end of the battlefield, the Federals, including the 20th Maine under Joshua Chamberlain, stopped the Confederates from overrunning Little Round Top.

During the evening, the soldiers of the 8th OVI heard the attacks on nearby Culp's Hill by General Richard Ewell's Confederate 2nd Corps. The Confederates were driven back, while Galwey and his comrades wondered about the outcome:

> *We who were out on the skirmish line heard a great deal of firing behind. Looking back we realized from the flashes of light, the roar of artillery, and the rattle of musketry, as well as by the much more convincing cheers that arose from time to time, that a desperate fight was going on behind us, over beyond the cemetery.*

Galwey learned that other regiments of his brigade had rushed to the Union defenses that night and driven the Confederates back. Galwey learned it had suffered forty-four casualties in this action.

Early in the morning of July 3, Galwey's company was ordered to advance again against Confederate skirmishers. Along with a New York regiment, they drove Confederate skirmishers from the Bliss barn, which the New Yorkers then burned down. In the midst of more firing, Galwey described how a Confederate sharpshooter got both sides to stop shooting in order to allow him to give water to a wounded Union soldier who lay between the lines. Then the fighting resumed. Galwey was given coffee while some of his company slept even amid more fighting.

Just before 1:00 p.m., the massive Confederate bombardment preceding their attack on Cemetery Ridge began. Galwey was hit twice by spent shell fragments, first in his foot and then in his thigh. The 8th OVI moved to a fence line out in front of the main Union line, with the right flank of the Federal army defending Cemetery Ridge. There they saw the advance of the Confederate 3rd Corps under General Johnston Pettigrew of North Carolina (later killed during Lee's retreat). This small regiment poured fire into the oncoming Rebels. They then began to retreat in disorder. The 8th OVI suffered in turn, with almost half of its small numbers becoming casualties. Galwey reported that of its 216 men, 103 were either killed or wounded (he himself was wounded), with the rest slightly wounded. Despite these tremendous casualties, they captured almost 200 Confederates and two of their battle flags.

Elsewhere, the Confederate assault was repulsed with massive casualties. At the Angle, Second Corps commander Hancock was wounded, and this wound plagued him during the rest of the war. The next day, as the opposing forces still faced each other, General Ulysses S. Grant's army marched into the Mississippi River stronghold of Vicksburg after its besieged garrison surrendered. That night, Galwey received his commission as a first lieutenant.

On July 5, Lee's shattered army began its retreat back to Virginia as the dead of both sides were buried. Overall, about fifty thousand combined were dead, wounded and missing/captured. Meade's army then began a fitful pursuit of Lee as President Lincoln urged Meade to deny another Confederate recrossing of the Potomac to safety. On July 13, Galwey's regiment found that the Confederates had successfully escaped at Falling Waters. Galwey expressed disappointment at Meade failing to attack Lee.

~~~

Despite the heroism of Irish American soldiers in the Hibernian Guard and the Irish Brigade at the Battle of Gettysburg, many Irish Americans rioted in July in New York City in protest at the draft. African Americans were targeted and suffered the highest death tolls. The city's police were unable to control the rioting mobs. Therefore, several regiments of the Army of the Potomac were sent to New York City to restore order. The 8th OVI arrived in New York Harbor on August 23, 1863. By then, the riots were over. Its stay in the city ended on September 7. Its time in New York was marred by occasional confrontations with "ruffians" and once in a brawl with some local police. There was also much drunkenness, including once by their commander, Franklin Sawyer. Galwey observed:

> *Generally, the people treat us well. That is to say, the moneyed people, those who are able to buy substitutes in case they are drawn in the conscription. But the poor, who have to fight in person, and not by hiring substitutes, look upon us with dislike, at least with suspicion, knowing that we were sent here to enforce the draft, which the riots in July had deferred.*

~~~

Upon arriving on September 11 at its camp in Northern Virginia, the regiment was met by election commissioners from Ohio with pamphlets from the gubernatorial candidates: Democrat Clement Vallandigham and Republican John Brough. All in Galwey's Hibernian Guards voted for Brough, even those under voting age like himself. Galwey confessed, "[W]e excused any irregularities in the mode of conducting the election as being a military necessity."

The next few months found Galwey and his company on skirmish duty. On October 2, Galwey was measured by the army's medical assistants. He weighed 146 pounds, and his height was five feet, six and three-fourth inches. The Second Corps was now commanded by General Gouverneur Warren, a hero of the Battle of Gettysburg, while General Hancock recovered from his wound. The corps found itself in combat again on October 14 with A.P. Hill's Confederate 3rd Corps as Hill attacked it at the Battle of Bristoe Station. Hill's attack was unsuccessful, for which he was reprimanded by Lee, and the Second Corps retreated across the Bull Run/Manassas battlefield.

On November 26, the 8th OVI reentered the Wilderness after crossing the Rapidan River. There they engaged in several skirmishes with Confederates, including cavalry led by General Wade Hampton. Galwey noted after one of these encounters with Confederates:

> *The effect of the enemy's peculiar, uncanny yelping upon our new men was very demoralizing. This cheer or hoot was taken, I believe from the Texas Rangers. It is always easy to know which side is advancing, by the character of the cheer. Ours was an unmistakable and prolonged hurra, whilst theirs was a succession of jerky, canine cries, which, at a distance, from its shrillness seemed like the sound of boys' voices, but when near it was terror-striking from its savageness.*

General Meade ordered the Second Corps to attack Lee south of the Chancellorsville battlefield. On November 30, 1863, as Galwey and his fellow soldiers prepared for the attack, General Warren surveyed the entrenched Confederates, decided that an attack would be futile and canceled the attack, ending Meade's short-lived offensive.

The Army of the Potomac went into winter quarters again. Galwey remembered a meeting of the Fenian Brotherhood of the Potomac Circle addressed by General Meagher of the Irish Brigade, the return of General Hancock and a deadly skirmish with Confederates. In February 1864, Galwey was once again assigned to recruiting duty, this time in Cleveland. During his weeklong stay there, he attended the Northern Ohio Sanitary Fair on Public Square. Galwey found:

> *And so the times passes, sometimes quickly, when I find the comforts of civil life very delectable. Then I think of my comrades back in Virginia and strangely enough I find my thoughts are with them even if my body is in Cleveland.*

~~~

Returning to his company's camp on May 2, 1864, Galwey found:

> *The company commander having lately sprained his ankle while playing football, was put in an ambulance and trundled back to the railroad company with the sick and infirm of the army, to be sent back to Washington. Thus I was left in command of the company.*

The greater military situation had also changed. While General George Meade still commanded the Army of the Potomac, President Lincoln had brought Ulysses Grant east to replace General Henry Halleck as commander of the Union armies. While in command now of all of the Union armies, Grant chose to accompany the Army of the Potomac as part of his coordinated plan for the spring campaigns in 1864. Meade's charge was to destroy Lee's army.

On May 3, 1864, Galwey, the 8th OVI and the rest of a vast Union army headed south. Grant's army once again entered the Wilderness and the Chancellorsville battlefield. In a repetition of the 1863 battle, Lee attacked Grant's army in the Wilderness beginning on May 5. The 8th OVI was in the thick of the fighting. Galwey described scenes of horror as the opposing armies fought in thick woods and wounded soldiers were threatened by forest fires. In this first battle of Grant's Overland Campaign, the Army of the Potomac suffered 17,600 casualties. Despite these losses, unlike previous commanders of this army, Grant did not retreat. Rather, on May 7, he raced south, trying to outflank Lee's army by capturing Spotsylvania Court House.

But on May 8, Union forces found the Confederates blocking them at Laurel Hill. The fighting would continue for almost two weeks. On May 10, General Emory Upton launched an innovative assault that at first succeeded but then was driven back. Savage fighting would take place at the "Bloody Angle" in what was called the "Mule Shoe." Galwey previously described this as exceeding in savagery all of the battles in which he fought. His brigade commander, General Samuel Carroll, commander of the 8th OVI back in 1861, had been wounded in the Wilderness battle, and now he was again seriously wounded, requiring the amputation of his left arm. Carroll's successor was killed. Galwey was again wounded, struck by a shell fragment in his leg. After treatment in a field hospital, Galwey rejoined his company. The Army of the Potomac experienced another thirty-six thousand casualties.

On May 15, two divisions of Hancock's corps moved south. Galwey reported:

> *I was detailed to command an outpost. Here the curious fact comes in, that I, a boy and merely a First Lieutenant, came into command of the regiment in this wise.…Our brigade commander, Carroll, had been wounded and disabled; our Lieutenant Colonel Franklin Sawyer, had been wounded and evacuated the same day; and every captain in the regiment without exception was absent—either killed, captured, wounded, or on leave of absence. Therefore, as I was the senior First Lieutenant of the regiment by virtue of date of commission, I assumed command of the regiment.*

While the 8th OVI saw action then and at the North Anna River (May 21–25), where another major battle was avoided, Grant again moved South to try to flank Lee's army. Galwey recounted the march of May 27:

> *Thus, since the 20th of May we have moved constantly by the left flank. I have been on many a hard, forced march, but this was one I would like to forget. Much of the time we were crossing ploughed fields and going up and down hills that were steep even if not high. Occasionally we waded through marshes, then for a short distance would be on a hard macadamized road. The first three hours of the march were made without a halt and almost at the double-quick. When it is remembered how hot it was, what loads we carried, and how little food we had had, something of the suffering of the men can be understood.*

As Grant's army approached Cold Harbor, the 8th OVI was informed that the end of its three-year enlistment was coming in June. Galwey confessed:

> *Some are talking of enlisting in another regiment. As for me, along with some of my friends I feel that the war is almost over and in all conscience we have done our part. I am in poor health besides having lost the use of one ear and am suffering from chronic dysentery.*

On June 3, 1864, Grant launched a massive attack at Cold Harbor that resulted in a loss that day of 5,600 Union casualties. Grant admitted in his memoir that he always regretted the last assault that day. While Hancock's corps was heavily engaged, Galwey's regiment was spared any great loss.

~~~

Grant stole a march on Lee and transported his army across the James River with the intention of capturing the railroad center of Petersburg. This would deny Lee of his major supply lines and force him out of the defenses of Richmond. Galwey's unit crossed the river on June 14. By June 17, 1864, Grant's army was arrayed before the Petersburg defenses, which had held against Grant's advance. Grant's army would not break through until April 2, 1865, after the defeat of George Pickett's force at Five Forks, which severed the last railroad line serving Lee's army. In the following week, the 8th OVI was engaged in more fighting:

> *At 7 a.m. on Friday, June 24, (this our last day in the war, we hope) the enemy opened his artillery all along the line, keeping up a heavy fire on us for an hour and a half but doing little damage. I am sure that many of my comrades would like to have dug themselves a deep hole on this their last day of active service. I am frank to admit that it wouldn't have been a bad idea; but at least we prayed that we would be saved to join our anxious families.*

That night, the 8th OVI received its mustering-out order to depart for Columbus, Ohio. Galwey ended his war diary thusly:

> *Strangely enough the word had already passed around, but there was little cheering, little celebration. We had expected to be transported with JOY. Perhaps soldiering in a splendid regiment is not so bad. Where would we find civilian friends to compare with soldier comrades?*

~~~

Galwey pursued his education and achieved four academic degrees, including a PhD. He mastered ten languages, including Latin and Greek. He eventually moved to Harlem in New York City and became a lawyer and educator (teaching logic and French literature at Manhattan College). He previously was an editor of a Cincinnati newspaper and another in Galveston, Texas. He became a lawyer for a department of the city of New York for twenty years. He married Mary Mitchell from Cincinnati in 1882, and they had four children. His son Geoffrey remembered him with his honorary military title of "Captain Brevet" in a biographical sketch:

Thomas Frances Galwey. *Courtesy of Jim Madden.*

Father was a well-known figure in Harlem and I can see him now returning to our Revolutionary War–vintage frame house on 129th Street, between Lennox and Fifth Avenue. It would be dusk and, as he marched—he never walked—with his cane carried like a sword, plus a bag of peanuts for the squirrels, he would be greeted by everyone. He would doff his derby with its fender-like brim, being a very polite man, and then he would come up the steps. Short and trim, acquiline of nose, deep-set blazing black eyes, black shaggy eyebrows, and snow-white hair.

As for his Civil War background:

He hated parades but he always took us to the Decoration Day parades and his sword cane would always be at his shoulder. One other weekly pilgrimage I'll always remember. His first sergeant in the Company B, the "Hibernian Guards," was Jim Butler, who became custodian of Grant's Tomb. My father would take us there on pleasant summer Sundays. Butler, wearing his Union uniform, a forage cap and blue coat, would treat us to plates of ice cream at a corner store, then would take us down to the crypt where the fabulous Grant lay. It always depressed me but I guess it was considered an honor.

Thomas Francis Galwey died on February 13, 1913.

The 8th OVI's perhaps best-known member was dentist Everton Conger, who accompanied the 16th New York Cavalry that cornered and killed Lincoln's assassin, John Wilkes Booth, in Northern Virginia. He carried Booth's diary to Secretary of War Ohioan Edwin Stanton. Conger first enlisted in the three-month 8th OVI but did not reenlist in the three-year 8th OVI. Instead, he next served in the 3rd (West) Virginia Cavalry and then the 1st District of Columbia Cavalry. The Union cavalry unit picked to hunt for Booth and his accomplice David Herold found them at the Garrett farm on April 26, 1865. Surrounded in a locked barn, the crippled Booth refused to surrender. Conger and his troops set fire to the barn. While the soldiers had been instructed to capture Booth, Sergeant Boston Corbett shot and killed him, claiming that God instructed him to act.

Corbett was a hatmaker who may have been poisoned by the mercury then used in hatmaking. As a member of the 16th New York Cavalry,

Corbett had been captured by John Mosby's rangers in Northern Virginia and imprisoned in the notorious Andersonville Prison in Georgia, but he was paroled in November 1864. Before and after the war, Corbett was an itinerant preacher. In 1874, Corbett arrived in Cleveland and worked in a hat factory. He preached in the old Methodist church at West Forty-Fifth Street and Bridge Avenue while residing in Cleveland. In September 1874, Corbett preached at a reunion of Union veterans at Caldwell, Ohio, which drew more than twenty thousand. Corbett didn't stay long in Cleveland. His travels eventually led him to Kansas, where Corbett disappeared in 1888.

John Wilkes Booth had Cleveland connections. He was one of America's most admired actors and performed in theaters across the county, including in Cleveland. In 1864, Booth turned to oil, forming the Dramatic Oil Company with two partners from Cleveland. One was John Ellsler, manager of the Cleveland Academy of Music. Their well in Pennsylvania failed to produce, and in September 1864, Booth gave up his oil holding. Long a Confederate sympathizer, instead of joining the Confederate forces, Booth formed a conspiracy to kidnap President Lincoln, taking him to Richmond and demanding the release of thousands of Confederate prisoners in exchange for his release. Booth was present at Lincoln's second inauguration. Later, he said that he could have killed him then.

With Lee's surrender and the Confederate government in flight, Booth's plans to kidnap Lincoln were no longer feasible. Instead, Booth was present (along with accomplices David Herold and Lewis Paine) on April 11, 1865, when Lincoln addressed a crowd from the White House. When Booth heard Lincoln endorse the idea of citizenry for the freed slaves, he responded, "That is the last speech he will ever make. Now, by God, I'll put him through." When Booth learned of Lincoln's plan to attend a play at Ford's Theatre on Friday, April 14, he put in motion a plan to murder Lincoln there and have co-conspirators also kill Secretary of State William Seward and Vice President Andrew Johnson. While Paine seriously wounded Seward, who was recovering from a serious injury, the would-be assassin of Johnson lost his nerve. Booth and Herold escaped, heading for southern Maryland and then northern Virginia, where they would finally be found.

A shocked nation, including the defeated Southerners and Northern opponents of Lincoln, soon learned of Lincoln's death on the morning of April 15. There was almost universal grief at Lincoln's death so soon after the end of the war that he had led that saved the Union. However, not all were sorry to learn of his assassination. In Cleveland on the afternoon of April 15 on Public Square, architect J.J. Husband said, "Lincoln's death was a damned small loss. While you have had your day of rejoicing, now I have mine. This is a good day for me." Overheard and pursued by an indignant crowd, Husband retreated to the office of the *Morning Leader* to deny his remarks and then went to his office to hide on the roof. The crowd found him there, threw him through a skylight and took him to the county courthouse. The next day, Husband escaped and left the city. Husband had designed the courthouse, which opened in 1858 and where the trials of the Oberlin-Wellington Rescuers were held. Following his escape, citizens removed Husband's name from the cornerstone of the courthouse that he had designed.

~~~

With a country in mourning, Lincoln's body (and that of his dead son Willie, who had died several years earlier) was placed on a funeral train for a return trip to Springfield for burial following in reverse the route that Lincoln took in 1861 to his inauguration. Following a funeral ceremony in Washington City, the Lincoln funeral train left on April 21 with Robert Lincoln, Lincoln's eldest son, initially accompanying the two bodies. One of the soldiers assigned to accompany the train was Clevelander George Elliot Sohl of the 124th OVI. His angry reaction to the assassination was to wish that now President Andrew Johnson should "totally exterminate the whole race of rebels." After his return to Washington City, Sohl was a guard at the prison holding the suspected assassins, whom he called "human fiends."

Huge crowds greeted the train where it stopped in cities, while other citizens stood by in tribute along the tracks as the train passed. Van Tassell and Vacha noted that Lincoln's train arrived in Cleveland on the rainy morning of April 28, 1865:

> *A military honor guard moved the coffin from the train to a hearse draped in black velvet with silver fringes and drawn by six white horses, each attended by a black groom. It proceeded down Euclid and was followed by Col. Oliver H. Payne, as assistant marshal. Various bands played dirges and a single cannon boomed on the half hour as the marchers solemnly made their way to Public Square.*

The coffin was placed on a catafalque called the "Pagoda Pavilion." Among other decorations on it was a streamer with a motto from the Roman poet Horace: *Extinctus amabitur idem* ("Dead, he will be loved the same").

The coffin was opened, and throughout the rainy day into the evening, an estimated 100,000 people viewed Lincoln's corpse. One of the onlookers, according to Dale Thomas, was Amelia Ames, whose husband was serving in the 124th OVI:

Amelia Ames stood watching the long procession at the corner of Erie (East Ninth) and Euclid Streets: "The slow-moving column of soldiers and citizens, the caisson draped, the muffled drums and solemn music of the band, the tolling bells, the firing of cannon, and the drooping of flags and banners with the misty rain falling softly. The President's remains were conveyed to a beautiful pavilion which had been erected on Public Square for the purpose. About eleven o'clock we fell into the citizen procession and about half past twelve looked upon the still, dead face of Abraham Lincoln."…After dinner, she returned to the Public Square and viewed the late president one last time…she again passed the Weddell

Abraham Lincoln's body on display in Public Square, Cleveland, Ohio. *Courtesy of Cleveland Memory Project, Michael Schwartz Library, Cleveland State University.*

House Hotel, where Lincoln had stayed overnight in February 1861: "We all sat up until eleven o'clock at night to see the procession leave. It passed down Superior Street directly by our windows and was another solemn as well as mournful spectacle. The whole street was lit up with torchlights carried by the escort, and as the funeral car passed, we could see it plainly. The rain was falling slowly but heavily, and the mournful music of the band did but add to the sadness in our hearts as we took one last look at the coffin which contained all that now remains of one whom we so loved to honor. It was a sight grand and at the same time sad, oh so sad and mournful. Long after we had retired to rest, the band in the street filled the air with solemn music, and muffled drums echoed like death upon our ears."

Late that night, the Lincoln funeral train departed for Columbus.

Grand Review of the Armies

On May 23–24, 1865, the eastern and western Union armies paraded through Washington City in the Grand Review before their volunteer soldiers were mustered out. On May 23, the Army of the Potomac was the first to march before the dignitaries and a huge crowd of admirers. Gettysburg hero Joshua Chamberlin observed:

At the head of the columns rode the cavalry regiments, at their post in the forefront, leading the army toward a destination....Behind the horsemen marched members of the provost marshal and engineer brigades. Then came the infantry, striding forth in files of twenty men across.

Ohio regiments mostly served in the western Union armies; 38, including the 37th OVI, were among the 178 regiments of General William Tecumseh Sherman's Western Army that passed in review on May 24:

Down the avenue poured the shining river of steel, gay with colors and rippling with cascades of mounted staff and burnished cannon. At the head proud, stern Sherman, who with thoughtful kindness had brought brave [General Oliver Otis] *Howard, now ordered to other duty, to ride by his side in this pageant. Following next is swarthy John Logan, leading the Army of the Tennessee, and* [General William] *Hazen with the*

Grand Review of Union armies. *Courtesy of Ohio History Connection.*

Fifteenth Corps. Each division is preceded by its corps of black pioneers, shining like polished ebony, armed with pick and spade, proud of their perfect alignment, keeping step to the music with inborn stress.

NOTABLE CLEVELAND PLACES

There are a few prominent places in Cleveland that have important connections to the events and some notable persons before, during and after the Civil War.

Public Square

When Moses Cleaveland's survey team laid out Cleveland in 1796, its central plaza modeled on the New England town square became Public Square. Over its more than two centuries, Public Square has seen many notable historical events. Just before the Civil War was the nearby trial of the Oberlin-Wellington Rescuers. During the war, regiments left from and returned to Public Square. Lincoln's funeral memorial was held on Public Square on April 28, 1865. In 1881, President James Garfield also was honored on Public Square by mourners before his funeral. In 1894, the Soldiers' and Sailors' Monument opened on Public Square.

Woodland Cemetery

With the Erie Street Cemetery in downtown Cleveland running out of space and surrounded by public streets, limiting the possibility of expansion, beginning in 1848 the city began looking for space to locate another public cemetery. Finally, in 1851, it was able to purchase sixty acres. The new cemetery was to be called Green Lawn Cemetery, but once it was designed, the city council decided to name it Woodland Cemetery because of its location in a wooded area. It opened on June 14, 1853.

With the outbreak of the Civil War, first the city donated a lot for the burial of Union soldiers, and in 1863 and 1868, the federal government purchased lots there to bury Union dead. Among the Union dead were William R. Creighton and Orrin J. Crane of the 7th OVI; General John J. Elwell of the 2nd Ohio Cavalry; William Henry Hayward and George W. Tibbetts of the 1st OVI, 103rd OVI and the 150th OVI; Thomas S. Paddock of the Cleveland Grays and the 150th OVI; and Staughton Bliss (assistant quartermaster of Ohio during the war).

Two regiments are honored with statues in the cemetery. First, a monument to the 23rd OVI, which fought at the battles of South Mountain and Antietam in western Maryland in September 1862, was authorized by Cleveland's city council in December 1862. The monument was dedicated on July 29, 1865, with Rutherford B. Hayes, future Ohio governor and U.S. president, who was wounded at South Mountain, speaking. This monument is considered to be the first regimental Civil War monument erected in the United States. On July 29, 2017, an Ohio historical marker was dedicated at the monument.

On Memorial Day 1872, a monument honoring the 7th OVI was dedicated at the cemetery.

7th OVI reenactors honor veterans buried at the Woodland Cemetery every Memorial Day. William R. Creighton and Orrin J. Crane are buried side by side in the cemetery. Creighton was a printer with the *Cleveland Herald* and raised a company that became Company A of the 7th OVI. He was

7th OVI Monument, Woodland Cemetery, Cleveland, Ohio. *Photo by Kay L. Martin.*

chosen to command the regiment in 1862. He was severely wounded in (West) Virginia. On November 27, 1863, at the Battle of Ringgold, Georgia, Creighton, then commanding a brigade, and Crane, then the commander of the 7th OVI, were both killed. There is a bust of Creighton in the Soldiers' and Sailors' Monument. Joseph B. Molyneaux of the 7th OVI is also buried there. He had two horses shot out from under him and was wounded twice at the Battle of Cedar Mountain on August 9, 1862, and he later served with the 150th OVI.

On June 24, 2012, a monument to the nearly eighty members of the U.S. Colored Troops (USCT) buried at Woodland Cemetery was dedicated. The monument is inscribed with the words of Frederick Douglass urging freed slaves to fight for the Union and also the names of those known members of the USCT buried there.

Lake View Cemetery

In 1869, some of Cleveland's civic leaders formed an association that purchased more than two hundred acres for a Lake View Cemetery. It was designed as a rural or garden cemetery. Among its prominent founders was Jeptha Homer Wade. He came to Cleveland from New York in 1856 and became wealthy through his role in the Western Union telegraph company. Wade was the cemetery's first president. Plots in the first section went on sale in 1870. The first person buried there was Louis Germain DeForest on August 25, 1870. Captain DeForest served with the 7th OVI. Mortimer Leggett, commander of the 78th OVI, is also buried there. After the war, he practiced law and was a member of the commission that planned the Soldiers' and Sailors' Monument, whose designer, Levi Schofield, is also buried there. Many of Cleveland's civic, business and political leaders, including several of those who have been profiled in this book, have been buried there. According to his wish, assassinated U.S. president James Garfield was buried there, and his memorial was also placed there.

THE ECONOMY AND POPULATION

Cleveland boomed during the Civil War. The clothing industry grew as ready-made clothing orders increased. Van Tassel and Vacha cite this:

Not long after Fort Sumter, a local clothing establishment appealed to rampant patriotism with what has been called the first jingle in local advertising:

Yes, we'll shout at Union Hall,
Where we clothe the people all…
And to Buckeye boys who go
We sell clothing very low.

The Cleveland Worsted Mill advertised for one thousand women to knit socks for Union soldiers. Iron and steel plants expanded. Stone, Chisholm & Jones built the first iron and steel blast furnace in 1861. By 1865, it was reported that more than half of the iron ore shipped from the Lake Superior mines came through Cleveland. Shipbuilding doubled, and four lake steamer lines had Cleveland offices. Oil refining expanded to thirty refineries by 1865. Three men exemplified the rise of manufacturing in Cleveland in this era: John D. Rockefeller, Henry Chisholm and Mark Hanna.

John D. Rockefeller

Rockefeller was born on July 8, 1839, in western New York. His father brought him to Cleveland in the fall of 1853. Grace Goulder noted:

The city to which young John D. Rockefeller had come was in a boom period of advancing prosperity. It had taken full advantage of its strategic location as a port both on Lake Erie and the Ohio Canal. The man-made waterway, credited with much of Cleveland's early growth, was giving way to the railroads. Yet the canal still functioned as an important carrier of manufactured goods going out from the city and produce coming in from lush farms in Ohio's countryside.

After finishing high school, Rockefeller gained employment on September 26, 1855, as a bookkeeper clerk with the commission merchants and produce shippers firm of Hewitt and Tuttle. On April 1, 1858, with money borrowed from his father, Rockefeller left the firm and joined Englishman Maurice B. Clark to form his own produce commission firm. Rockefeller was a fervent member of the Erie Street Baptist Church, whose members included Benjamin and Rebecca Rouse and Henry Chisholm, who in 1863 would organize the Cleveland Rolling Mill company.

With the advent of the Civil War, Rockefeller and Clark prospered. When President Lincoln called for volunteers in the spring of 1861, Rockefeller did not answer the call. He was against slavery and voted for Lincoln in 1860, but Rockefeller said:

> *I wanted to go into the army and do my part. But it was simply out of the question. We were in a new business and if I had not stayed it must have stopped—and with so many dependents.*

Rockefeller supported his family, while his youngest brother, Frank, at age sixteen, enlisted in the 7th OVI. Frank was wounded twice during the war. Meanwhile, John paid the $300 to hire a substitute, although he did provide support to some Union soldiers. When Lieutenant Levi Schofield brought thirty recruits into Rockefeller's office in August 1862, Rockefeller reached into a big bag of money from the safe and handed each recruit $10 for enlisting in the 103rd OVI.

On August 28, 1859, in Titusville in western Pennsylvania, a well drilled by Edwin Drake gushed oil, and a drive began to replace other fuels. Oil soon began to arrive in Cleveland. Samuel Andrews, an Englishman and friend of Maurice Clark, became interested in the oil business and approached Clark and Rockefeller about forming a partnership to refine oil. Rockefeller had visited Titusville and the oil fields in 1860. In November 1863, a rail connection was established between Cleveland and the western Pennsylvania oil fields. Tensions arose between Rockefeller and Andrews wanting to expand their business, with Clark resisting them. While their original firm grew and made Rockefeller wealthy, he eventually decided that he could no longer partner with Clark. On March 2, 1865, after dissolving the firm and buying out his partner, Rockefeller assumed control of what became Rockefeller and Andrews, which began with its Excelsior Oil Works on Kingsbury Run. Rockefeller would go on to monopolize the oil refining industry with the creation of Standard Oil and become the wealthiest man in the United States. According to his biographer Ron Chernow:

> *Thus, by the end of the Civil War, John D. Rockefeller had established the foundations of his personal and professional life and was set to capitalize on the extraordinary opportunities beckoning him in postwar America.*

While a student at Cleveland's Central High School, Rockefeller had befriended Laura Celestia Spelman, known as "Cettie." The Spelmans were abolitionists, and while living in Akron, their home served as a station on the Underground Railroad. Returning to Cleveland after college, Cettie became a public school teacher. With his increasing prosperity as a businessman, Rockefeller pursued a reluctant Cettie; in early 1864, they became engaged. They were married in secrecy in the Spelman family house on September 8, 1864. From a mansion on Millionaires Row on Euclid Avenue in downtown Cleveland, Rockefeller eventually began to live primarily in a former summer house at Forest Hill, four miles east of his downtown Cleveland residence. In 1883, Rockefeller and his Standard Oil Company moved to New York City.

John D. Rockefeller. *Courtesy of Ohio History Connection.*

Henry Chisholm

Henry Chisholm, known as the "father of the Cleveland steel industry," emigrated from Scotland to Montreal, Canada, in 1842. He had been a carpenter since he apprenticed at the age of twelve. In 1850, Chisholm came to Cleveland to work on building a breakwater at the Lake Erie terminal of the Cleveland & Pittsburgh Railroad. In 1857, Chisholm began the rolling steel firm of Chisholm Jones & Company. Renamed Stone, Chisholm & Jones Company after Andros Stone, the younger brother of Amasa Stone, invested in the firm in 1858, it erected the first blast furnaces in Northeast Ohio in 1859. In 1863, Chisholm created the Cleveland Rolling Mill Company. It built the second Bessemer steel processing plant in the United States in 1865.

Mark Hanna

Another notable Cleveland industrialist was Marcus "Mark" Hanna. He attended Cleveland Central High School at the same time as John

D. Rockefeller. He went into his family's business, which was similar to Rockefeller's first business firm. During the Civil War, Hanna, like Rockefeller, paid for a substitute. His brother Howard served in the navy. Mark Hanna did join a regiment of the Ohio National Guard, which was temporarily sent to Washington City in the summer of 1864 to guard it against Confederate general Jubal Early's threatened attack. However, Hanna had returned to Ohio and did not see any military action. Oliver Payne, commander of the 124th OVI, expressed a low opinion of Hanna, "undoubtedly colored by Hanna's avoidance of military service." Hanna married the daughter of wealthy Cleveland businessman Daniel P. Rhodes and joined his iron business, which eventually was named M.A. Hanna & Company.

Van Tassel and Vacha cited this statistic, which showed the impact of manufacturing growth in Cleveland during the Civil War:

> *According to the Cleveland Board of Trade, the value of all Cleveland manufacturing rose during the Civil War from $7 million in 1860 to $39 million in 1865.*

According to the entry on "Cleveland in the Civil War" in the *Encyclopedia of Cleveland History*:

> *Historian Crisfield Johnson has best summarized the war's local impact: "…the war found Cleveland a commercial city and left it a manufacturing city. Not that it ceased to do a great deal of commercial business, but the predominant interests had become the manufacturing ones."*

Like Johnson, Phyliss Anne Flower also concluded:

> *Thus, one may say that at the outbreak of the Civil War the city of Cleveland was a commercial and trading center, but the war years provided the necessary impetus to carry the city through a successful transition period in its growth from a commercial terminus to a thriving industrial center. The demands of the war upon Cleveland industries awakened businessmen to the realization that the future of the city depended upon the maintenance and development of the iron mills and foundries rather than an emphasis on commerce.*

By 1866, Cleveland's population had increased to more than 67,500 (an increase of more than half since the 1860 census count).

Post–Civil War Cleveland

The Fenian Invasion of Canada

After the Civil War, some Irish American Union veterans joined the Fenian movement, dedicated to liberating Ireland from British rule. To forward this ultimate goal, the Fenians decided to invade Canada to end British rule in North America. In May 1866, however, they abandoned the original plan to cross Lake Erie from Cleveland led by a veteran who had headed the 58th Illinois Volunteer Infantry. Instead, a train left Cleveland on May 29 headed for Buffalo with 340 Fenians of the Irish Republican Army aboard. On June 2, 1866, they crossed the Niagara River to invade Canada. They were met by Canadian forces and soundly defeated at the Battle of Bridgeway on June 2, 1866; 14 Fenians, including 4 from the Cleveland Rangers regiment, were killed, and 117 were captured. The Cleveland Rangers were led by Irish-born John Grace, who served in the 34th OVI during the Civil War.

The U.S. government intervened to try to prevent any further Fenian incursions into Canada. In September 1867, a wing of the Fenian Brotherhood met in Cleveland and pledged to mount another Canadian invasion. On May 25, 1870, several hundred Fenians crossed the border at St. Albans, Vermont. Compromised by a spy, they were easily defeated at the Battle of Eccles Hill. On May 27, a second small force of Fenians crossed the border at Malone, New York, where they were met by British regulars from Montreal and quickly defeated at the Battle of Trout River, as noted by Klein.

The Irishmen who had picked up rifles at Eccles Hill and Trout River longed to be bathed in glory. Instead, they departed from the Canadian border in a shower of ridicule. Newspapers giddily printed the joke that the "I.R.A." emblazoned on the buttons of the Fenians' green jackets stood, not for the "Irish Republican Army," but for their new motto—"I Ran Away."

RECONSTRUCTION

The daunting question facing the country after the Civil War was what would be the fate of the millions of emancipated slaves. The Radical Republicans in Congress, led by Representative Thaddeus Stevens and Senator Charles Sumner, sought citizenship and equality for them. Abraham Lincoln's successor as president, Andrew Johnson, was a southerner who held very racist views. The federal government did create a Freedmen's Bureau to provide some assistance to the former slaves.

A political battle erupted over a proposed Fourteenth Amendment to the Constitution to grant citizenship to the former slaves. In 1866, Congress passed a civil rights bill over a veto by President Johnson. In opposition, Johnson conducted a speaking tour (called the "Swing around the Circle"), which included a speech in Cleveland. This was followed by passage of the Fourteenth Amendment. The author of its Equal Protection Clause was Ohio lawyer and congressman John Bingham. He had been a prosecutor of Lincoln's assassins. While Johnson also opposed the amendment, the Republican Congress in 1867 required that the representatives of the former Confederate states could only be re-admitted to Congress if their states ratified the Fourteenth Amendment. This resulted in its ratification in July 1868. That same year, President Johnson was impeached but escaped conviction by a single vote. General Ulysses S. Grant succeeded him as president.

In 1870, the Fourteenth Amendment was also ratified, giving Black males the right to vote. In the South, Black citizens exercised their new right to vote, and many were elected to local, state and even federal offices. This led to a White backlash. The Ku Klux Klan formed to terrorize the former slaves and prevent their voting. The Republican Congress responded with federal troops to maintain law and order. It also passed an 1871 law to prosecute the Klan, which President Grant used to protect Black citizens.

The efforts of White southern leaders, many of whom were ex-Confederate soldiers and politicians, to regain political supremacy came to a head in the 1876 presidential election. New York Democratic governor Samuel Tilden was the apparent winner over Ohio Republican governor and wartime general Rutherford B. Hayes. However, the Republicans disputed the results in three southern states won by Tilden. Congress then established an Electoral Commission (which included James Garfield and Cleveland lawyer and Democratic politician Henry Payne) to investigate and determine the winner. By partisan votes, the commission ruled 8-7 in each case for Hayes, giving him an Electoral College victory of 185-184.

Shortly after his inauguration, Hayes withdrew the remaining federal troops from the South. This enabled the White Democratic Party in the South to regain control of its governments and deny Black citizens voting rights and economic progress. This began the decades of racial segregation and under the "Jim Crow" laws and violence against the former slaves and eventually the Great Migration North of southern Blacks to northern cities, including Cleveland.

CLEVELAND'S RISE AS AN INDUSTRIAL CITY

Building on its growth during the Civil War, Cleveland continued its expansion of industrialized manufacturing after the war. The Cleveland Rolling Mill Company led the way in steel. In 1868, it installed a pair of Bessemer converters to produce steel. The company prospered, but in 1882, its workers, both the skilled (mostly British) and unskilled (Polish and Czech), organized to demand a closed shop, which would set workers' pay scales. The company's president, William Chisholm (Henry's brother), rejected the workers' demands. A strike ensued, and the company hired unskilled Polish and Czech strikebreakers. Violence ensued in June 1882, and the strike collapsed that July. In the summer of 1885, another strike occurred when the company cut wages in the midst of a business recession. Led by Polish and Czech strikers, the company shut down. In July, a riot broke out as the strikers shut down mills. Cleveland's mayor ordered Chisholm to restore the wage cut, and that ended the strike, although the company refused to rehire many of the strikers.

In 1883, a novel entitled *The Bread-Winners* was published anonymously. It described labor strife in a fictional Cleveland and took an anti-union position. Its author was John Hay, although he denied writing it. Hay had married Clara Stone, the daughter of Cleveland millionaire industrialist Amasa Stone, in 1874. Hay was known as one of President Abraham

Lincoln's secretaries during the Civil War and coauthor of his multi-volume biography. Hay would later become a diplomat and secretary of state for Presidents William McKinley and Theodore Roosevelt.

Along with the steel industry and iron ore, oil refining became a major part of Cleveland's industry. Dominating it was John D. Rockefeller's firm. In December 1865, his firm inaugurated a second refinery in Cleveland, the Standard Works. In 1867, Rockefeller hired Henry M. Flagler at the demand of Steven V. Harkness, a wealthy Cleveland businessman who invested heavily in the new firm of Rockefeller, Andrews and Flagler. During the Civil War, Flagler had prospered initially as a grain contractor for the Union armies. In 1868, Rockefeller and Flagler negotiated the first of the railroad rebates that would mark the rise of Standard Oil. In 1870, the partnership was converted into the Standard Oil Company. In 1872, during February and March, Rockefeller bought out almost all of his oil refinery competitors in what became known as the "Cleveland Massacre." One of the Cleveland firms that Rockefeller bought was owned by Oliver Hazard Payne, who commanded the 124th OVI during the Civil War. Payne then became an officer of Standard Oil and a very wealthy man. Standard Oil's campaign to create a monopoly continued in other cities. With his success, in 1883 Rockefeller and his family moved to New York City. He also moved the headquarters of Standard Oil to New York City.

Rockefeller would go on to become the wealthiest American of his time. His Standard Oil Company would become the target of muckraking journalist Ida Tarbell, and it would eventually be broken up under the Sherman anti-trust law. After his wife Cettie's death in 1913, Rockefeller became embroiled in a dispute over taxes that Cuyahoga County claimed he owned as a resident. After arranging to secretly bury his wife at Cleveland's Lake View Cemetery, Rockefeller mostly cut his personal ties to Cleveland. He did make some charitable contributions there, including land for the Forest Hill and Rockefeller Parks. Rockefeller died in 1937 and was buried with family members at Lake View Cemetery.

After the Civil War, and after some initial setbacks, Mark Hanna became a very successful businessman. He also became involved in Republican politics. He supported James Garfield's 1880 presidential campaign, and after his assassination, Hanna presided over his funeral arrangements. Hanna eventually became a friend of then Ohio governor William McKinley and assisted him financially during the Panic of 1893. Hanna managed McKinley's successful 1896 presidential campaign, raising large amounts of money to elect him. In 1897, Hanna was appointed a U.S. senator by the

Ohio General Assembly to take the seat vacated by John Sherman, whom he had supported for the Republican presidential nomination in 1888. He managed McKinley's successful 1900 reelection campaign. Hanna died in 1904 during the presidency of McKinley's successor, Theodore Roosevelt. A statue of Hanna by Augustus Saint-Gaudens sits in Cleveland's University Circle neighborhood.

By 1884, Cleveland's board of trade was reporting that there were 147 businesses in Cleveland manufacturing iron and steel and their products. They were employing European immigrants coming to Cleveland to work in their factories and shops.

Mass Immigration

Previously, the Germans and the Irish were the two most numerous European immigrant groups to come to Cleveland. During the post–Civil War decades of industrialization, they were followed by waves of immigrants from southern, central and eastern Europe. They came to escape conditions in the "old country" and mostly to find work. In Cleveland, the unskilled immigrants worked in the mills and shops, the port and the railroads, while more skilled workers fared better in the city's growing economy. Most lived in overcrowded housing in ethnic neighborhoods near to where they worked. With their arrivals, the city's population grew tremendously: 1870—92,829; 1880—160,140; 1890—261,353; and 1900—381,768.

Garfield Memorial

As a politician in the postwar era, Ohio congressman James Garfield gained in stature and influence. He served on the Electoral Commission that decided the 1876 presidential election in favor of Ohio governor Rutherford B. Hayes. As the Republican presidential nominating convention of 1880 approached, Garfield supported Ohio senator John Sherman. The convention was virtually deadlocked between the candidacies of James Blaine and Ulysses Grant (seeking a third term), representing two rival factions of the Republican Party. On the thirty-sixth ballot, the convention instead threw its support to Garfield.

Garfield narrowly defeated fellow Union general Winfield Scott Hancock to win the presidency. Tragically, on July 2, 1881, Garfield was shot by a disappointed office seeker. Garfield lingered until September 19, when he finally died from his wound. He was returned to Cleveland for burial. A public viewing was held on Public Square, attended by an estimated 250,000 mourners. The U.S. Marine Band played "In Memoriam President Garfield's Funeral March," a funeral dirge composed by its director, John Philip Sousa. Sousa had previously composed "President Garfield's Inauguration March."

James A. Garfield. *Courtesy of Ohio History Connection.*

Following President James Garfield's death, a committee was formed to plan a memorial. After an international competition was held and a designer chosen, construction began on October 6, 1885. The Garfield Memorial opened in Lake View Cemetery on Memorial Day 1890. The slain president is commemorated by a statue, and his tomb is within the memorial. There are five bas-reliefs with life-size figures depicting Garfield's many roles in life, including his military service in the Civil War, and also some famous Americans, including Presidents Hayes and Arthur. Within recent years, there has been extensive restoration work done on its structure and façade.

Daniel Vermilya concluded:

> *James Abram Garfield was a man made both by and for the Civil War. His life story, rising from the poverty of a log cabin to the presidency, was only possible in the Union that he and so many others fought to save. He was a volunteer soldier and officer in a volunteer war. His story is in many ways the story of the Union. Though not perfect, he came from the most humble beginnings, and through the fiery trial of the Civil War, he rose to a position of leadership in a bold new era of American history. The war saw James Garfield go from the role of a college instructor and state legislator to the halls of the United States House of Representatives, the platform on which he would eventually prove himself worthy of the presidency. The men who emerged as leaders of the United States in the decades after the Civil War were those who largely achieved their roles because of what they had done for their country during that conflict. Just as the war transformed the United States, it transformed the lives of those who lived it, endured it and experienced it as well.*

In 1876, Garfield acquired and enlarged a house in Mentor, east of Cleveland. During his front porch presidential campaign in 1880, it became known as Lawnfield. In 1980, Congress made Lawnfield a National Historic Site.

SOLDIERS' AND SAILORS' MONUMENT

On October 22, 1879, Civil War veteran William J. Gleason, who served in the 150th OVI, proposed the building of a monument to honor the Union soldiers and sailors from Cuyahoga County. While there was widespread agreement with this idea, it took some time to win agreement on its future location on Public Square. This was finally resolved with the southeast quadrant becoming its site.

The architect chosen to design the monument was Levi Schofield, a veteran who enlisted in the 1st Ohio Light Artillery (Battery D) and later served in Company E of the 103rd OVI and on the staff of Ohioan General Jacob Dolson Cox. Schofield's grandfather came to Cleveland from New York City in 1816. In 1856, Schofield's father built the Schofield Block. As an architect, Levi Schofield was known for his institutional buildings.

The memorial hall of the monument is decorated with several relief sculptures, including one depicting "Lincoln Freeing the Slave." Another commemorates the Soldiers' Aid Society, with several women pictured, including Rebecca Rouse. There is also a bust of Clevelander General James Barnett.

Towering above the building is a column inscribed with the names of battles in which the veterans fought. Atop it is the fifteen-foot-tall Lady Liberty, with a sword in her right hand. It is thought that the model for her was Schofield's wife, Elizabeth.

Atop each side of the building are sculptures created by Schofield depicting groups representing the army, navy, artillery, cavalry and most especially the nine-man color guard of the 103rd OVI, all of whom were killed or wounded at the Battle of Resaca, Georgia, in May 1864.

The base building of the monument is a memorial hall that contains the names of the Cuyahoga County Union veterans. On June 19, 2019, thanks to the efforts of a history schoolteacher and his students, the names of 107 members of the U.S. Colored Troops (USCT), which had been found, were to be added to the names of 23 other local members of the U.S. Colored Troops.

Right: Soldiers' and Sailors' Monument, Public Square, Cleveland, Ohio. *Photo by Kay L. Martin.*

Below: The color guard, Soldiers' and Sailors' Monument, Public Square, Cleveland, Ohio. *Photo by Kay L. Martin.*

The Soldiers' and Sailors' Monument was dedicated on July 4, 1894, with a huge crowd in attendance. The keynote speaker was the veteran of the 23rd OVI, Ohio governor and future U.S. president William McKinley.

GRAND ARMY OF THE REPUBLIC

In 1866, Union veterans led by former Major General John Logan, one of its founders, formed the Grand Army of the Republic (GAR), in which most veterans became members. Its local and state posts held regular reunions, as did the national organization. There were a number of GAR posts in Cleveland and Cuyahoga County. Three GAR national encampments were held in Cleveland. The sixth was held in Cleveland in 1872. The thirty-fifth was held in Cleveland in September 12–13, 1901, attended by more than thirty thousand veterans. The third held in Cleveland was the eighty-first, held in August 1947, when there were very few Union veterans still alive. The last surviving GAR member in Cuyahoga County, Peter Diemer, a Clevelander born in 1844 who served with the 150th OVI, died on February 23, 1943. The major legacy of the GAR was the establishment by John Logan in 1868 of Decoration Day (now Memorial Day) annually on May 30 to commemorate the Union dead. At the first Decoration Day on May 30, 1868, James Garfield spoke at Arlington National Cemetery.

CONCLUSION

The Civil War had a profound impact on Cleveland. Thousands of its citizens rallied to the support of the Union by enrolling in its armed forces, including in the military units profiled here. Many of them were killed and wounded. The families of those who served were likewise deeply affected, especially if their family members were casualties. Clevelanders on the homefront organized support for the soldiers and sailors, most notably the Soldiers' Aid Society.

Cleveland's economy boomed, as did its population, fueled by advances in manufacturing that would continue into the postwar decades as the city became an industrial powerhouse. The most notable industrialist to emerge in Cleveland during the Civil War was John D. Rockefeller, the creator of the Standard Oil Company monopoly that would make him the wealthiest American.

The Civil War experience of those Clevelanders who served in the Civil War, both in the military and in supporting organizations, has been remembered in monuments. Most notably are the Soldiers' and Sailors' Monument, located on Public Square, and the President James Garfield Memorial, located at Lake View Cemetery. In addition to those who served in the military and supported them, Clevelanders paid tribute at Public Square to two assassinated presidents of the United States, James Garfield and Abraham Lincoln.

BIBLIOGRAPHY

Abbott, Richard H. *Ohio's Civil War Governors*. Columbus: Ohio State University Press, 1962.

Achorn, Edward. *Every Drop of Blood: The Momentous Second Inauguration of Abraham Lincoln*. New York: Atlantic Monthly Press, 2020.

Ackerman, Kenneth. *Dark Horse: The Surprise Election and Political Murder of President James A. Garfield*. N.p.: Viral Press, 2011.

Armstrong, William H. *Major McKinley, William McKinley & the Civil War*. Kent, OH: Kent State University Press, 2000.

Baumgartner, Richard A. *Buckeye Blood at Gettysburg*. Huntington, WV: Blue Acorn Press, 2003.

Bellesiles, Michael A. *1877: America's Year of Living Violently*. N.p.: The New Press, n.d.

Bernstein, Iver. *The New York City Draft Riots: Their Significance for American Society and Politics in the Age of the Civil War*. New York: Oxford University Press, 1990.

Bilby, Joseph G. *The Irish Brigade in the Civil War: The 69th New York and Other Irish Regiments of the Army of the Potomac*. Boston, MA: Da Capo Press, 2001.

Billings, John D. *Hardtack & Coffee: The Unwritten Story of Army Life*. Omaha: University of Nebraska Press, 1993.

Bissland, James H. *Blood, Tears, & Glory: How Ohioans Won the Civil War*. Wilmington, OH: Orange Frazer Press, 2007.

Brands, H.W. *The Zealot and the Emancipator: John Brown, and the Struggle for American Freedom*. New York: Doubleday, 2020.

Brandt, Nat. *The Town that Started the Civil War*. Syracuse, NY: Syracuse University Press, 1990.

Castel, Albert. *Decision in the West: The Atlanta Campaign of 1864*. Lawrence: University Press of Kansas, 1992.

Catton, Bruce. *Grant Moves South*. Boston: Little Brown and Company, 1960.

———. *Mr. Lincoln's Army: The Odyssey of General George Brinton McClellan and the Army of the Potomac*. Garden City, NY: Doubleday & Company, 1951.

———. *A Stillness at Appomattox*. Garden City, NY: Doubleday & Company, 1953.

Chamberlain, Joshua Lawrence. *The Passing of the Armies: An Account of the Final Campaign of the Army of the Potomac, Based Upon Personal Reminiscences of the Fifth Army Corps*. Reprint, New York: Bantam Books, 1993. Originally published in 1915.

Chernow, Ron. *Titan: The Life of John D. Rockefeller, Sr.* New York: Vintage Books, 1998.

Chester, H.W. *Recollections of the War of Rebellion: A Story of the 2nd Ohio Volunteer Cavalry, 1861–1865*. Edited by Alberta R. Adamson. Wheaton, IL: Wheaton History Center, 1996.

Cleveland Historical. "Civil War Cleveland." https://clevelandhistorical. org/tours/show/19.

Cornish, Dudley Taylor. *The Sable Arm: Negro Troops in the Union Army, 1861– 1865*. New York: Longmans, 1956.

Cowsert, Zac. "Righteous or Riotous? The 2nd Ohio Cavalry and the Crisis." *Civil War Discourse: A Civil War Era Blog*, November 30, 2015. http://www. civildiscourse-historyblog.com/blog/2015/11/30/righteous-or-riotous-the-2nd-ohio-cavalry-and-the-crisis.

Cozzens, Peter. *The Shipwreck of Their Hopes: The Battles for Chattanooga*. Urbana-Champaign: University of Illinois Press, 1996.

———. *This Terrible Sound: The Battle of Chickamauga*. Urbana-Champaign: University of Illinois Press, 2016.

Crenshaw, Douglas. *Fort Harrison and the Battle of Chaffin's Farm: To Surprise and Capture Richmond*. Charleston, SC: The History Press, 2013.

Crowl, Thomas. *Opdycke's Tigers in the Civil War: A History of the 125th Ohio Volunteer Infantry*. Jefferson, NC: McFarland & Company, 2019.

Day, Michelle, and Gail Chambers. *Woodland Cemetery*. Images of America series. Charleston, SC: Arcadia Publishing, 2013.

Day, Michelle, and Joseph Wicken. "The Arrest and Trial of Lucy Bagby." Cleveland Historical. https://cleveland historical.org/items/show/517.

Decaro, Louis A. *The Untold Story of Shields Green: The Life and Death of a Harper's Ferry Raider*. New York: New York University, 2020.

Dee, Christine. *"Feel the Bonds that Draw": Images of the Civil War at the Western Reserve Historical Society.* Kent, OH: Kent State University Press, 2011.

Fearing, Heidi, and Chris Roy. "Camp Cleveland." Cleveland Historical, 2011. https://clevelandhistorical.org/items/show/314

Flower, Phyllis Anne. "Cleveland, Ohio, During the Civil War." MA thesis, Ohio State University, 1940.

Foner, Eric. *The Second Founding: How the Civil War and Reconstruction Remade the Constitution.* New York: W.W. Norton & Company, 2019.

Galwey, Thomas. *The Valiant Hours: Narrative of "Captain Brevet," an Irish-American in the Army of the Potomac.* Edited by W.S. Nye. Harrisburg, PA: Stackpole Company, 1961.

George, Harold A. *Civil War Monuments of Ohio.* Lakewood, OH: Harold A. George, 2006.

Glatthaar, Joseph. *Forged in Battle: The Civil War Alliance of Black Soldiers and White Officers.* New York: Free Press, 1990.

————. *The March to the Sea and Beyond: Sherman's Troops in the Savannah and Carolinas Campaigns.* New York: New York University Press, 1985.

Goodwin, Doris Kearns. *Team of Rivals: The Political Genius of Abraham Lincoln.* New York: Simon & Schuster, 2005.

Goulder, Grace. *John D. Rockefeller: The Cleveland Years.* Cleveland: Western Reserve Historical Society, 1972.

Groom, Winston. *Shrouds of Glory: From Atlanta to Nashville: The Last Great Campaign of the Civil War.* New York: Pockets Books, 1995.

Hatch, Thom. *Glorious War: The Civil War Adventures of George Armstrong Custer.* New York: St. Martin's Press, 2013.

Heineman, Kenneth J. *Civil War Dynasty: The Ewing Family of Ohio.* New York: New York University Press, 2013.

Hess, Earl J. *Storming Vicksburg: Grant, Pemberton, and the Battles of May 19–22, 1863.* Chapel Hill: University of North Carolina Press, 2021.

Hoptak, John David. *The Battle of South Mountain.* Charleston, SC: The History Press, 2011.

Horwitz, Lester V. *The Longest Raid of the Civil War.* Cincinnati, OH: Farmcourt Publishing, 1999.

Horwitz, Tony. *Midnight Rising: John Brown and the Raid that Started the Civil War.* New York: Henry Holt and Company, 2011.

Jordan, Brian Matthew. "'The Regiment Bore a Conspicuous Part': A Brief History of the Eighth Ohio Volunteer Infantry, Gibraltar Brigade, Army of the Potomac." *Gettysburg Historical Journal* 5, no. 6 (2007).

Keating, Dennis. "The 8th Ohio Volunteer Infantry." Cleveland Civil War Roundtable, 2012. https://www.clevelandcivilwarroundtable.com/the-8th-ohio-volunteer-infantry.

Kendrick, Paul, and Stephen Kendrick. *Douglass and Lincoln: How a Revolutionary Black Leader and a Reluctant Liberator Struggled to End Slavery and Save the Union.* New York: Walker Publishing Company, 2008.

Kern, Albert. *History of the First Regiment, Ohio Volunteer Infantry in the Civil War, 1861–1865.* Dayton, OH: A. Kern, 1918.

Kimberly, Robert, and Ephraim S. Holloway. *History of the 41st Ohio Veteran Volunteer Infantry.* Huntington, WV: Blue Acorn Press, 1999.

Klein, Christopher. *When the Irish Invaded Canada: The Incredible True Story of the Civil War Veterans Who Fought for Ireland's Freedom.* New York: Doubleday, 2019.

Lazette, Michelle Park. "Camaraderie Drives Local Civil War Re-enactors." *Crain's Cleveland Business,* April 8, 2017.

Lewis, George W. *The Campaigns of the 124th Regiment, Ohio Volunteer Infantry, with Roster and Roll of Honor.* Akron, OH: Werner Company, 1894. Reissued by Project Guttenberg EBook, 2016, available at https://www.gutenberg.org/files/52223/52223-h/52223-h.htm.

Lewis, Thomas A. *The Guns of Cedar Creek.* New York: Harper & Row, 1988.

Magliocca, Gerald N. *American Founding Son: John Bingham and the Invention of the Fourteenth Amendment.* New York: New York University Press, 2016.

Martelle, Scott. *The Madman and the Assassin: The Strange Life of the Man Who Killed John Wilkes Booth.* Chicago: Chicago Review Press Inc., 2017.

Maryniak, Benedict. "The Fenian Raid and Battle of Ridgeway June 1–3, 1866." University at Buffalo, State University of New York. http://www.acsu.buffalo.edu/~dbertuca/155/FenianRaid.html.

Matter, William D. *If It Takes All Summer: The Battle of Spotsylvania.* Chapel Hill: University of North Carolina Press, 1988.

McPherson, James M. *For Cause & Comrades: Why Men Fought in the Civil War.* New York: Oxford University Press, 1997.

Mezurek, Kelly D. *For Their Own Cause: The 27th United States Colored Troops.* Kent, OH: Kent State University Press, 2015.

Mieyal, Timothy J. "A Story of Valor: The Seventh Ohio Voluntary Infantry." MA thesis, Kent State University, 1996.

Noyalas, Jonathan A. *The Battle of Cedar Creek: Victory from the Jaws of Defeat.* Charleston, SC: The History Press, 2009.

Oates, Stephen B. *Our Fiery Trial: Abraham Lincoln, John Brown, and the Civil War Era.* Amherst: University of Massachusetts Press, 1983.

———. *Woman of Valor: Clara Barton and the Civil War*. New York: Free Press, 1995.

Ohio History Central. "William C. Quantrill." https://ohiohistorycentral. org/w/william_C._Quantrill.

Pacini, Lauren R. *Honoring Their Memory: Levi T. Schofield, Cleveland's Monumental Architect and Sculptor*. Cleveland, OH: Artography Press, 2019.

Pawlak, Kevin R., and Dan Welch. *Ohio at Antietam: The Buckeye State's Sacrifice on America's Bloodiest Day*. Charleston, SC: The History Press, 2021.

Perdue, Theda. "Stand Watie's War: The Last Confederate General." HistoryNet. https://www.historynet.com/stand-waties-war-the-last-confederate-general.htm.

Pershey, Edward J. "Cleveland, Ohio, and Lincoln's Assassination and Funeral." Ford's Theatre. https://www.fords.org/blog/post/cleveland-ohio-and-lincolns-assassination-and-funeral.

Reynolds, David S. *John Brown, Abolitionist: The Man Who Killed Slavery, Sparked the Civil War, and Seeded Civil Rights*. New York: Vintage Reprint, 2006.

Rose, William Ganson. *Cleveland: The Making of a City*. Cleveland: World Publishing Company, 1950.

Ross, D. Reid. "Civil War Grand Review." HistoryNet. https://www. historynet.com/civil-war-grand-review.htm.

Sawyer, Franklin. *A Military History of the 8th Regiment, Ohio Volunteer Infantry: Its Battles, Marches and Army Movements*. N.p., 1881. Reprinted as *8th Ohio Volunteer Infantry: Gibraltar Brigade, Army of the Potomac*. Huntington, WV: Blue Acorn Press, 1994.

Schmiel, Eugene D. *Citizen-General: Jacob Dolson Cox and the Civil War Era*. Athens: Ohio University Press, 2014.

Schultz, Jane. *Women at the Front: Hospital Workers in the Civil War*. Chapel Hill: University of North Carolina Press, 2007.

Sears, Stephen W. *Gettysburg*. Boston: Houghton Mifflin Company, 2003.

———. *Landscape Turned Red: The Battle of Antietam*. Boston: Mariner Books, 1993.

Siedel, Paul. "Peter Diemer & Curtis Phillips: The Last Civil War Veterans from Cuyahoga County." Cleveland Civil War Roundtable, 2016. https:// www.clevelandcivilwarroundtable.com/peter-diemer-curtis-phillips-the-last-civil-war-veterans-from-cuyahoga-county.

Smith, Timothy B. *The Union Assaults at Vicksburg: Grant Attacks Pemberton, May 17–22, 1863*. Lawrence: University Press of Kansas, 2020.

Soldiers' and Sailors' Monument. http://www.soldiersandsailors.com.

Stark, William C. "History of the 103rd Ohio Volunteer Infantry Regiment, 1862–1865." MA thesis, Cleveland State University, 1986.

Still, John S. *The Life of Rufus Spalding: An Ohio Politician*. Columbus: Ohio State University Press, 1948.

Stocker, Jeffrey. "118 Overlooked Ohio Gunners Made a Difference at Gettysburg." HistoryNet, July 21, 2020. https://www.historynet.com/118-overlooked-ohio-gunners-made-a-difference-at-gettysburg.html.

Swanson, James L. *Bloody Crimes: The Chase for Jefferson Davis and the Death Pageant for Lincoln's Corpse*. New York: HarperCollins, 2010.

Taliaferro, John. *All the Great Prizes: The Life of John Hay, from Lincoln to Roosevelt*. New York: Simon & Schuster, 2014.

Tenney, Frances Delia Andrews. *War Diary of Luman Harris Tenney, 1861–1865*. Cleveland, OH: Evangelical Publication House, 1914. Reprinted by Wentworth Press, 2016.

Thomas, Dale. *Civil War Soldiers of Greater Cleveland: Letters Home to Cuyahoga County*. Charleston, SC: The History Press, 2013.

Trudeau, Noah Andre. *Southern Storm: Sherman's March to the Sea*. New York: HarperCollins, 2008.

Tuve, Jeanette E. *Old Stone Church: In the Heart of the City Since 1820*. Virginia Beach, VA: Donning Company, 1994.

Van Tassel, David D. *The Encyclopedia of Cleveland History*. Edited by John J. Grabowski. Bloomington: Indiana University Press, 1987. https://case.edu/ech/articles/c/civil-war.

Van Tassel, David D., and John Vacha. *Behind Bayonets: The Civil War in Northern Ohio*. Kent, OH: Kent State University Press, 2006.

Vermilya, Daniel J. *James Garfield and the Civil War: For Ohio and the Union*. Charleston, SC: The History Press, 2015.

Vorhees, Catherine Durant. *The Colors of Dignity: The Memoirs of Brigadier General Giles Waldo Shurtleff*. N.p.: self-published, 2013.

Vourlojianis, George N. *The Cleveland Grays: An Urban Military Company, 1837–1919*. Kent, OH: Kent State University Press, 2002.

Washington, Versalle F. *Eagles on Their Buttons: A Black Infantry Regiment in the Civil War*. Columbia: University of Missouri Press, 1999.

Waugh, John C. *Reelecting Lincoln: The Battle for the 1864 Presidency*. New York: Crown Publishers, 1997.

Weiser-Alexander, Kathy. "The Civil War in West Virginia." Legends of America, November 2018. https://www.legendsofamerica.com/civil-war-west-virginia.

Welch, Daniel. "My Favorite Historical Person: Thomas Francis Galwey." Emerging Civil War, June 10, 2017. https://emergingcivilwar.com/2017/06/10/my-favorite-historical-person-thomas-francis-galwey.

Wert, Jeffry D. "George Custer: Facts, Information and Articles About George Custer, a Civil War General during the Civil War." HistoryNet. https://www.history.net.com/george-custer.

———. *The Sword of Lincoln: The Army of the Potomac.* New York: Simon & Schuster, 2005.

Western Reserve Historical Society. Civil War Manuscripts Collection. Cleveland, Ohio. wrhs.org.

Wheelan, Joseph. *Bloody Spring: Forty Days that Sealed the Confederacy's Fate.* Boston, MA: Da Capo Press, 2014.

White, Jonathan W. *Emancipation, the Union Army, and the Reelection of Abraham Lincoln.* Baton Rouge: Louisiana State University Press, 2014.

Widmer, Ted. *Lincoln on the Verge: Thirteen Days to Washington.* New York: Simon & Schuster, 2020.

Wiley, Bell Irvin. *The Life of Billy Yank: The Common Soldier of the Union.* Garden City, NY: Doubleday & Company, 1971.

Williams, T. Harry. *Hayes of the Twenty-Third: The Civil War Volunteer Officer.* New York: Alfred A. Knopf, 1965.

Wittenberg, Eric, Edmund A. Sargus and Penny L. Barrick. *Seceding from Secession: The Civil War, Politics, and the Creation of West Virginia.* Eldorado Hills, CA: Savas Beatie, 2020.

Woodworth, Steven E. *Six Armies in Tennessee: The Chickamauga and Chattanooga Campaigns.* Omaha: Bison Books/University of Nebraska Press, 1999.

INDEX

A

Antietam 39, 40, 58, 63, 64, 67, 82,
  83, 86, 90, 91, 109
Army of the Potomac 40, 41, 57,
  60, 75, 77, 82, 83, 87, 88, 89,
  90, 91, 92, 93, 95, 96, 98, 99,
  100, 107
Atlanta (Georgia) 34, 37, 39, 40,
  44, 49, 62, 69, 70, 72, 74, 77, 90

B

Bagby, Sara Lucy 27, 28
Barnett, James 77, 123
Barton, Clara 43, 44
Battle of Buffington Island 64
Battle of Chancellorsville 59, 94
Booth, John Wilkes 14, 27, 103,
  104
Brown, John 16, 17, 18, 21, 23, 25,
  27

B

Burnside, Ambrose 47, 64, 91, 92,
  93

C

Camp Cleveland 14, 42, 43, 44
Chancellorsville 77, 83, 94, 96, 99,
  100
Chase, Salmon P. 21, 23, 25, 32,
  34, 35, 36, 40, 68, 86
Chattanooga 41, 60, 63, 69, 72
Chickamauga 40, 41, 63, 67, 68,
  69, 73, 74
Cleveland Grays 30, 43, 55, 62, 77,
  86, 109
Cleveland Herald 21, 51, 58, 109
Cleveland Leader 29, 46, 57
Cleveland Plain Dealer 29, 35
Compromise of 1850 15, 20
Cox, Jacob Dolson 39, 40, 42, 63,
  70, 123
Crane, Orrin J. 58, 60, 109, 111

Creighton, William 58, 60, 109, 111
Custer, George Armstrong 40, 75, 76, 77
Cuyahoga County 14, 23, 27, 28, 29, 32, 35, 38, 42, 55, 67, 70, 71, 77, 120, 123, 125

D

Douglass, Frederick 21, 25, 36, 78, 111
Douglas, Stephen 16, 17, 18, 28, 29, 30, 33
Dred Scott decision 18

E

Elwell, John J. 43, 44, 74, 109
Emancipation Proclamation 21, 91

F

Fort Sumter 51, 62, 86, 112
Fredericksburg 83, 87, 88, 92, 93, 94
Frémont, John C. 17, 36, 37, 41, 88
Fugitive Slave Act 15, 16, 20, 23, 27

G

Galwey, Thomas Francis 57, 82, 83, 84, 86, 87, 88, 89, 90, 91, 92, 93, 94, 95, 96, 97, 98, 99, 100, 101, 102, 103

Garfield, James 13, 14, 19, 36, 41, 54, 63, 68, 69, 109, 111, 119, 120, 121, 122, 123, 125, 127
Gettysburg 39, 40, 59, 77, 83, 84, 86, 96, 98, 99
Grand Army of the Republic 14, 72, 125
Grand Review of the Armies 44, 75, 77, 107
Grant, Ulysses S. 34, 39, 40, 41, 72, 84, 97, 100, 101, 102, 103, 118, 121

H

Hanna, Mark 27, 56, 112, 114, 115, 120, 121
Harper's Ferry 18, 25, 91
Hayes, Rutherford B. 47, 63, 64, 65, 67, 90, 109, 119, 121, 122
Hibernian Guards 56, 57, 62, 82, 86, 87, 96, 98, 103
Hooker, Joseph 59, 90, 93, 94, 95

I

Irish Brigade 57, 90, 92, 93, 98, 99

J

Jackson, Thomas "Stonewall" 37, 58, 82, 88, 91, 94
Jim Crow 119
Johnson, Andrew 37, 104, 105, 118

K

Kansas-Nebraska Act 16, 17
Kennesaw Mountain 63
Ku Klux Klan 118

L

Lake View Cemetery 111, 120,
    122, 127
Lee, Robert E. 25, 34, 42, 59, 82,
    88, 89
Lincoln, Abraham 13, 14, 15, 17,
    18, 21, 28, 29, 30, 31, 32, 33,
    34, 35, 36, 37, 38, 41, 42, 51,
    55, 56, 62, 74, 75, 77, 78, 83,
    87, 89, 90, 91, 92, 93, 94, 95,
    98, 100, 103, 104, 105, 106,
    107, 109, 113, 118, 120, 123,
    127

M

McClellan, George 32, 33, 35, 38,
    39, 40, 41, 86, 88, 89, 90, 91,
    130
McKinley, William 63, 64, 120,
    121, 125
Meade, George 95, 100
military units
    1st OLA 70, 77, 84
    1st OVI 57, 62, 63, 109
    2nd OVC 74, 75, 76, 77
    5th USCT (125th OVI) 77, 78,
        80
    7th OVI 58, 60, 62, 68, 109, 111,
        113
    8th OVI 57, 82, 83, 84, 86, 87, 88,
        89, 90, 91, 92, 95, 96, 97, 98,
        99, 100, 101, 102, 103
    23rd OVI 41, 63, 64, 67, 90, 109,
        125
    37th OVI 38, 71, 72, 107
    41st OVI 46, 63, 72, 73, 74
    103rd OVI 35, 42, 46, 47, 57, 70,
        71, 90, 109, 113, 123
    124th OVI 45, 46, 49, 67, 69, 105,
        106, 115, 120
    125th OVI 73, 77
    150th OVI 55, 109, 111, 123, 125
Missionary Ridge 60, 63, 69, 72
Morgan, John Hunt 33, 57, 64, 74

O

Oberlin College 20, 21, 23, 25, 27,
    39, 58, 75, 76, 78, 80, 82, 105,
    109
Oberlin-Wellington Rescue 20, 21
Ohio State Penitentiary 64
Orchard Knob 63

P

Public Square 14, 21, 28, 32, 45,
    51, 54, 60, 70, 99, 104, 105,
    106, 108, 122, 123, 127

R

Reconstruction 118
Resaca 63, 70, 123
Ringgold Gap 60

Rockefeller, John D. 13, 19, 27, 30, 62, 112, 113, 114, 115, 120, 127
Rosecrans, William 41, 42, 68, 69
Rouse, Rebecca 51, 53, 54, 113, 123

W

Woodland Cemetery 27, 60, 62, 67, 109, 111

S

Schofield, Levi 14, 70, 111, 113, 123
Shenandoah Valley 37, 39, 40, 58, 75, 76, 82, 87, 88
Sherman, William T. 32, 34, 37, 39, 40, 44, 47, 60, 62, 69, 70, 72, 73, 74, 80, 107, 120, 121
Shiloh 41, 63, 68, 73
Soldiers' Aid Society 50, 51, 53, 54, 123, 127
Soldiers' and Sailors' Monument 14, 28, 34, 53, 70, 77, 109, 111, 123, 125, 127
Spotsylvania Court House 84, 86, 100
Stone's River 41, 63, 74
Stowe, Harriet Beecher 16, 20

U

Uncle Tom's Cabin 16, 20
Union Depot 43, 44, 70

V

Vallandigham, Clement 27, 29, 34, 35, 98

ABOUT THE AUTHOR

W. Dennis Keating is an Emeritus Professor who taught in the Levin College of Urban Affairs and the Cleveland-Marshall College of Law at Cleveland State University. He has written widely about urban planning, urban policy, neighborhoods and housing. His publications about Cleveland include the 2016 History Press book *A Brief History of Tremont: Cleveland's Neighborhood on a Hill*. He is a past president of the Cleveland Civil War Roundtable and has written numerous articles for its newsletter, *The Charger*. Two of his ancestors served in the 168th and the 206th Pennsylvania Volunteer Infantry regiments during the Civil War.